OREGON ROAD TRIPS

NORTHEAST EDITION

MIKE & KRISTY WESTBY

Mosier Tunnel Photo Copyright Ian Poellet
Bridal Veil Falls Photo Copyright Megan Westby
The vast majority of photos contained herein are © Mike Westby

Active, Oregon™

Discover Scenic Backroads & Byways by Day,
Stay in Historic Hotels by Night™

ISBN-13: 978-0998395005

010119 - CS

Cover design by Sarah Craig – SarahCookDesign.com

"Oregon is where summer comes to play."

Follow
Discover-Oregon

On the Web:
www.Discover-Oregon.com

On Twitter:
@DiscoverOre.com

On Facebook:
www.Facebook.com/DiscoverORE

On Instagram:
DiscoverOregon4300

OREGON ROAD TRIPS
NORTHEAST EDITION

Discover Northeast Oregon!

An exciting 9-day vacation exploring Northeast Oregon's scenic backroads & byways is now as easy as 1-2-3...

1) Write in the Dates of Your Trip

2) Make Your Historic Hotel Reservations

3) Pack Your Bags and Go!

With this easy-to-use guide, you'll simply turn each page as you motor along and choose which points of interest to stop at and explore during your day's journey, *all while making your way towards an evening's lodging at a historic Oregon hotel.*

An exciting adventure awaits...and it's already planned for you!

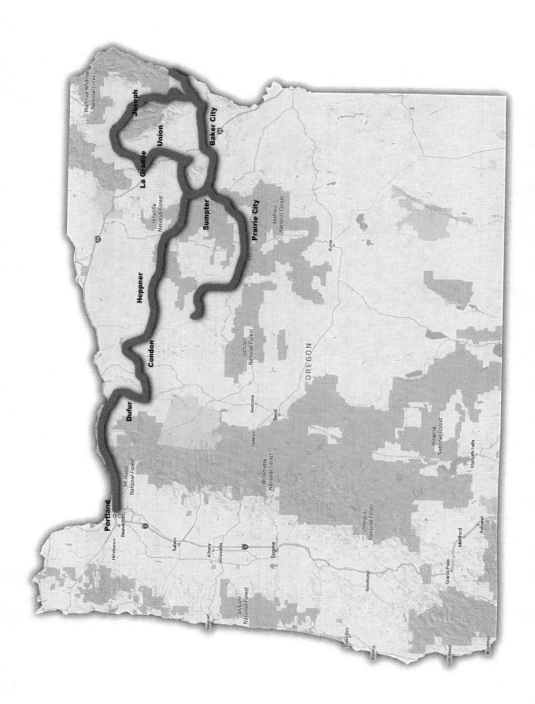

YOUR JOURNEY

INTRODUCTION

Oregon is a vast and beautiful state. I could list its square mileage, its demographics or perhaps the distance from border to border, but a better description is...it starts with the shores of the Pacific Ocean on its western edge, traverses east over the Oregon Coast Range and into the verdant Willamette Valley, climbs over the snowy summits of the Cascade mountain range while skirting south of the sublime Columbia River Gorge and then continues forever into the remote, silent and dramatic beauty and history of eastern Oregon.

This guide is about setting out on your own adventure to explore Oregon. It's about the journey, not the destination. It's about asking, "I wonder what that is?" It's about hitting the brakes and turning left off the pavement. Opening a door and saying "Hello". Shutting off the engine, getting out of the car and listening to the silence of distance, punctuated only by crickets and the occasional call of a Meadowlark. It's about the angry tug on a fly line, wondering just how many stars a sky can hold and what would really happen, I mean *really* happen, if you just kept going.

Recently, my wife, Kristy, and I set out on a nine-day 1,400 mile journey along the backroads and byways of northeast Oregon to discover its intriguing sites, small towns and scenic wonders, all while staying in historic hotels each evening. Our goal was to stop and explore all of the places we normally rush past when we're traveling because we're in such a hurry to reach our destination. As we met people along the way, we were surprised by the number of folks who said they've always wanted to make a similar trip but they didn't know where or how to begin planning it, and this was usually followed by a request for a copy of our itinerary and notes once we finished our journey. We decided to go one step further and write up our notes, add our photos, include some maps and turn it all into an easy-to-use book so that others could duplicate our trip with little effort, all while customizing it to their own interests and sense of adventure.

HOW TO BEGIN

Oregon's immense size, historical treasures and abundance of geographical features are too much to capture in one trip. In fact, its countless riches can be so intimidating that travelers don't know where to begin...so they don't.

Good news! This book already has your route planned for you. There are only three simple things you need to do...

1) Select the 9-day period for your trip and write those dates into this book at the beginning of each chapter.

2) Call and make reservations at the historic hotels found at the end of each day, which correspond with your chosen dates.

3) Pack your bags, hop in the car and simply choose the sights you wish to stop at and explore each day as you motor along.

Note that some of the optional activities you'll enjoy during your trip, such as the Columbia River Sternwheeler, Sumpter Valley Railroad Train or Sunrise Iron Antique Tractor Collection, will also require reservations, and these are noted at the beginning of each chapter/day.

WHERE TO START

Your 9-day road trip begins in Portland *or* Hood River and proceeds in a clockwise direction through the northeast portion of the state.

Two Starting Points

1) If you choose to begin from Portland, simply start your journey at Day 1 on Page 20.

2) If you are coming from the east and do not wish to travel to Portland to begin your trip, then travel to Hood River, Oregon and begin there, part way through Day 1.

In addition, with a little ingenuity on your part, you could actually begin this trip at any point along its 9-day clockwise journey. Simply write in your dates, make the corresponding historic hotel reservations and begin.

www.Discover-Oregon.com

MAKE YOUR RESERVATIONS

Ride the Sumpter Valley Railroad – Day 5

These are the reservations you will need to make for your trip. All necessary lodging reservations are shown in bold. All others are optional activities.

Day 1 – Columbia River Gorge to Dufur, OR

- **Historic Balch Hotel - 541-467-2277**
- Columbia River Sternwheeler - 503-224-3900

Day 2 – Dufur, OR to Condon, OR

- **The Hotel Condon - 541-384-4624**

Day 3 – Condon, OR to Baker City, OR

Choose your lodging for 2 nights: (Days 3 & 4)

- **Geiser Grand Hotel, Baker City, OR – 541-523-1889**
  or
- **Wisdom House, Baker City, OR – VRBO #: 726034**

Day 4 – Explore Baker City, OR

- No reservations required today

Day 5 – Baker City, OR to Union, OR

- **Historic Union Hotel - 541-562-1200**
- Sumpter Valley Railroad Steam Train - 541-894-2268

Day 6 – Union, OR to Joseph, OR

Choose your lodging for 3 nights: (Days 6, 7 & 8)

- **1910 Historic Enterprise House** B&B - **541-426-4238**
  or
- **Bronze Antler Inn - 541-432-0230**
  or
- **Wallowa Lake Lodge & Cabins - 541-432-9821**

- Eagle Cap Excursion Train - 800-323-7300
- Sunrise Iron Antique Tractor Collection:
  541-426-4407 or 541-263-0755
  Reservations are preferred but not required

Day 7 – Explore Joseph, OR

- Joseph Branch Rail Riders - 541-786-6149
- Valley Bronze Foundry Tour - 541-432-7445

Day 8 – Explore the Zumwalt Prairie Preserve

- No reservations required today

Day 9 – Joseph, OR to Prairie City, OR

- **Historic Hotel Prairie - 541-820-4800**
- Hells Canyon Jet Boats - 541-785-3352

SOME GROUND RULES

"It's the Journey, Not the Destination."

The key to your journey is to alter your driving mindset. It really isn't about getting *there*, it's about discovering *here*. With this in mind, here are some ground rules to follow...

- Get used to stopping the car and getting out.
- Now stop the car and get out.
- Stop the car and get out...again. You'll be glad you did.
- Always ask "I wonder where that goes?"...and go there.
- Hit the brakes and turn left.
- Open the door and say "Hello."
- Don't assume it has to be a short conversation.
- Never mind that you just stopped back there...stop again here.
- Yes, it is a nice view. You should stop, get out and admire it.
- Always remember that this very moment is the time to do it. You won't be coming back this way next week.
- Enjoy the journey!

It Doesn't Have to Be 9 Days

We've laid out an exciting 9-day road trip for you, but don't feel you have to adhere to that schedule. Want a shorter trip? Then simply head home sometime mid-journey. Want to spend more time on the road? Then feel free to stay an extra night in a town or two of your choice.

Travel Beyond the Page

By all means, do not feel you have to stop at only the places found in this book, as there are many more than those listed here just waiting to be discovered. Go ahead...follow that dusty road, stop at that small museum, visit the town's old cemetery, and walk that trail to the viewpoint. It's all about taking the time to...discover Oregon.

"So, Where Are You From?"

There are many blessings on a trip like this, one of which is the number of conversations you simply fall into. It usually begins with a simple question or comment, and the next thing you know, you're involved in a 30-minute conversation with some of the nicest people you've ever met. Why? Because the folks you meet on a trip like this are your neighbors, it's just that they're a quite a few houses further down the block. If you approach a town, café, museum or someone with an air of traveling arrogance, then you're making a huge mistake. Instead, be genuine and friendly. You'll be amazed at how many people you'll meet and how pleasant your trip will be.

And in those rare instances where you meet someone who loves to talk...about themselves...then excuse yourselves with the tried and true "Well, we need to be hitting the road if we're going to stay on schedule."

The Right Frame of Mind

During your journey, your mindset will make all the difference between having an amazing trip filled with fond memories that will last a lifetime or a less-than-stellar odyssey you'd just as soon forget. Is the single-pane window in your 1920s era hotel room a bit drafty? Then it's historically accurate, not in need of replacement. Did you come out to your car one morning only to find a flat tire? Find a helpful Les Schwab Tire Store and be thankful it's not a broken spoke on a wagon wheel. Did the Haines Steakhouse close early because it was kind of slow today? Then that's exactly the taste of the slower pace of life you were seeking. Always go with the flow, and you'll be happy you did.

Get Some Good *Paper* Maps

We can't emphasize this enough. You will want to travel with and use a couple of good paper maps, and the more detailed, the better. Your phone or similar device will no doubt work well, but you're setting out to explore some remote parts of Oregon, many of which have no cell signal whatsoever, so your phone will not work there. In addition, your paper maps will always boot up and never run out of power.

As you make your way along your journey and stop at various locations, you'll often see folded Oregon maps made available for free by the Oregon Department of Transportation. These are very helpful, so grab more than one and keep them with you at all times. For more fine detail on the backroads you'll be traveling, we also recommend the large Oregon atlases put out by DeLorme, which you can find online for about $25.

Oregon's tourism division, Travel Oregon, also issues very helpful maps, magazines and trip guides. We highly recommend you visit their web site, www.TravelOregon.com, to order some of these guides before setting out on your trip. Especially helpful is their large *Oregon Scenic Byways Official Driving Guide.*

If you are a member of AAA, check their resources, as well. By the way, make sure your membership is up-to-date.

The Time of Year Makes a Difference

Your Discover Oregon journey is a trip best made during mid-spring to late fall, when temperatures are warm, the days are longer and the alpine roads are clear of snow and winter debris. Most roads are open year-round, but portions of the higher elevation scenic byways, such as the Blue Mountain Scenic Byway, Elkhorn Drive Scenic Byway and Hells Canyon Scenic Byway, are still closed due to snow in early to mid-spring. Plan on most routes being snow free sometime in mid- to late May, though this can vary. If you're traveling during this time, call the corresponding Ranger Stations to get the latest road status. Travel tools, such as a small shovel and bow saw, may come in handy when traveling early in the year.

Note that the mid-summer months of July and August can be very warm in the central and northeast sections of Oregon, with temperatures sometimes reaching well into the 90s.

Be Prepared

Be self-sufficient as you travel along, as some areas are quite remote. Be sure to bring extra food, drinks, a first-aid kit, a roadside emergency kit, a phone charger with cables, a tire inflator, (yes, I've had to use one!) a blanket, maps, a small shovel, flashlights with fresh batteries, a lighter, a whistle, road flares and a small tarp to sit upon should you have to change a tire or dig out from some snow. Note that should you experience some kind of difficulties while on the road, chances are someone will be along soon.

Six Hours Per Day – Your Results May Vary

As we've said, it's all about the journey and not the destination. That said, we found that after about six hours of being on the road, we were flipping this mantra and were ready to reach our destination. Our willingness to stop and explore was being replaced by a desire to simply reach our hotel, relax and "be there." Everybody's results will certainly vary, but we found that about six hours on the road was enough for a day.

Antique Typewriters

Long ago abandoned is the antique typewriter, the turn-of-the-prior-century "computer". It seems every museum, historic hotel, restaurant, and antique store you'll walk into during your journey has one. The goal is to find it and be the first to do so.

Take Your Time and Enjoy the Sights

 As you make your way through this book, you'll see a small clock icon placed next to some of the listings. There are many attractions that do not require much time to visit. A stop at the Vista House may require about half an hour, while a stop at Rowena Crest may require half that, but locations and attractions such as the Wallowa Lake Tramway, the Sumpter Valley Railroad, and the Joseph Branch Railriders absolutely call for you to spend more time enjoying these once-in-a-lifetime experiences. Wherever you see the clock icon, plan on spending at least an hour at that location, and we would encourage you to spend even more time there while hiking to a waterfall, exploring an interpretive center, or even riding aboard a sternwheeler. If it means missing out on some of the other stops, then so be it. They'll be waiting for you on your next trip to Northeast Oregon!

What Caused the Fire?

As you make your way along the western end of the Historic Columbia River Highway, you'll notice obvious signs of a large fire that swept through the area, as evidenced by swaths of trees with blackened trunks, chainsawed tree stumps, and dying trees covering nearby hillsides and distant ridges.

In September of 2017, a 15 year-old boy carelessly tossed a lit firework into dry grass and leaves while hiking in the Columbia River Gorge and set off a massive wildfire that burned for weeks, closed I-84 for an extended period, forced the evacuation of hundreds of people from their homes, destroyed many historic trails and structures in the Gorge, and consumed nearly 50,000 acres of forest land. Thankfully, only 15% of that area was rated as "Highly Burned".

Thanks to the brave efforts of hardworking firefighters and emergency responders, as well as countless volunteers and citizens of communities throughout the Columbia River Gorge, most of the Gorge was saved from this devastating wildfire, and today trails are being reopened, bridges are being rebuilt, and the burned areas are again springing to life.

www.Discover-Oregon.com

DAY ONE

HISTORIC COLUMBIA RIVER HIGHWAY SCENIC BYWAY

PORTLAND TO DUFUR, OR

"Discovery is an adventure. There is an eagerness, touched at times with tenderness as one moves into the unknown. Walking the wilderness is indeed like living. The horizon drops away, bringing new sights, sounds and smells from the earth."

William O. Douglas (1898-1980)

Day 1
Portland to Dufur, OR

Day 1 – Date: /   /

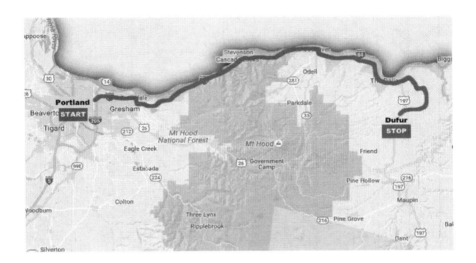

Summary: Where You're Going Today:

- Portland, OR
- Columbia River Gorge
- Crown Point
- Cascade Locks, OR
- Hood River, OR
- Rowena Crest
- The Dalles, OR
- Dufur, OR

Today's route travels the Historic Columbia River Highway Scenic Byway along the northern border of Oregon, taking you from Troutdale to Cascade Locks, on to Hood River and then out to Rowena Crest and The Dalles before finishing at the historic Balch Hotel in the small town of Dufur. Today will be a long day with plenty to do, so you'll want to get an early start.

Tonight's Lodging:

- The Historic Balch Hotel

Today's Mileage: 98 Miles

Reservations Needed for This Segment:

- Historic Balch Hotel - 541-467-2277
- Columbia River Sternwheeler - 503-224-3900

Start

Your Northeast Oregon Road Trip begins in Troutdale, OR. To get there...

- Travel I-84 East from Portland and take Exit 17.

- Continue straight from the exit for 0.7 mile to Graham Road. Turn right here and follow this south for 0.3 mile to the Columbia River Highway / Historic Route 30. Turn left / east here, where you'll then pass under the large "Gateway to the Gorge" sign.

- You are now on the Historic Columbia River Highway Scenic Byway and beginning your road trip into the Columbia River Gorge and Northeast Oregon.

Note that the small shops and restaurants you're passing here in Troutdale make for an excellent stop for breakfast or to grab a cup of coffee for your travels this morning.

The Columbia River Gorge

The Columbia River Gorge is a natural wonder of sublime grandeur filled with elegant and majestic waterfalls, towering geological features, endless vistas, and fields of colorful spring wildflowers that bloom from mid-February through June, and then dry in the summer winds before welcoming autumn's fiery oranges, reds and yellows.

As you travel the Historic Columbia River Highway Scenic Byway, you will pass countless waterfalls, hikes, vistas and historical points of interest. We could include many of them here, but then that would make this a Columbia River Gorge trail guide, filling three quarters of the book. For an excellent resource on the abundance of Columbia River Gorge trails and viewpoints, we highly recommend the book *Curious Gorge*, by Scott Cook. You'll find it in shops during your road trip.

☐ Your First Stop: Rail Depot Museum – Depot Park

Railroads have played a very important role in Oregon's history, and their history in the Gorge runs back to before the turn of the 20th century. In fact, later today in Cascade Locks, you'll see the Oregon Pony, the very first steam locomotive used in the Oregon Territory. For now, you'll visit Troutdale's Rail Depot Museum. Originally built in 1882 and rebuilt in 1907 after it burned, the museum offers visitors a look at just how the depot appeared when it was in use in the early 1900s. In addition, rail fans will find a nicely restored Union Pacific caboose in the parking lot.

Rail Depot Museum
473 E. Historic Columbia River Highway
Troutdale, OR 97060
503-661-2164

- Open: Every Friday from 10:00 a.m. to 2:00 p.m.

Driving Directions: From the "Gateway to the Gorge" sign, travel east for 0.2 miles, where you'll find the entrance to the museum on your left.

☐ Next Stop: Barn Exhibit Hall

The large Barn Exhibit Hall features changing exhibits which tell of the rich history of Troutdale and the surrounding area. Currently, visitors will find an impressively curated exhibit marking the 100th anniversary of the Historic Columbia River Highway, the first highway in the United States to be built as a scenic road, as well as the first to include a painted center line!

Barn Exhibit Hall
732 E. Historic Columbia River Highway
Troutdale, OR 97060
503-661-2164

- Open: Wednesday through Saturday – 10:00 a.m. to 3:00 p.m., Sunday – 1:00 p.m. to 3:00 p.m.

Driving Directions: From the Rail Depot Museum, continue along the Columbia River Highway for 0.2 miles to The Barn Exhibit Hall on your right.

▢ **Next Stop:** Crown Point Vista House

Offering a commanding view into the heart of the Columbia River Gorge at the west end of the old Columbia River Highway, the Crown Point Vista House is one of Oregon's classic historical icons. Built atop a massive basalt promontory in 1917, its unique stone structure is "a temple to the natural beauty of the Gorge." Inside, travelers will find a museum showcasing the history of the building and the Columbia River Gorge, as well as a small gift shop, restrooms, and a café serving coffee.

Crown Point Vista House
40700 E. Columbia River Highway
Corbett, OR 97019
503-344-1368

- Open Daily: 9:00 a.m. – 4:00 p.m.
- Closed if winds exceed 50 mph or if there is snow or ice.

Driving Directions: From the Barn Exhibit Hall, continue on the Columbia River Highway for 0.4 miles, where you'll take a right turn after crossing a narrow bridge over the Sandy River. Continue from here for 9.5 miles to the Vista House.

Note that at the 8.7 mile mark from the bridge you'll see a road for Larch Mountain veering off to the right. This destination is not on today's journey, but if you were to come this way again and follow this for 14 miles to the "summit" of Larch Mountain, you'd find a large parking area with a path leading to a viewpoint which offers a commanding "reach out and touch it" view of Mt. Hood. Note that this road is closed from late fall to early spring. It is also a popular road with cyclists.

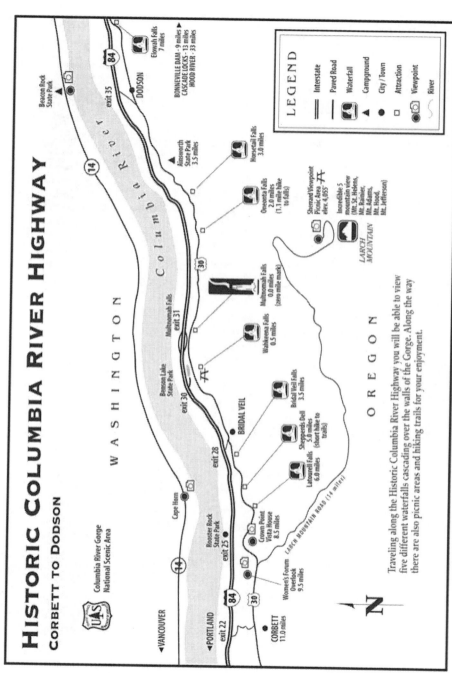

Map courtesy of Friends of Multnomah Falls

Columbia River Gorge Waterfalls

The Columbia River Gorge is home to over two dozen beautiful waterfalls close to the highway, with Multnomah Falls being by far the most popular. Appearing one after the other as you motor along, stop and visit any one of them along this stretch of the Historic Columbia River Highway. Many, such as Latourell Falls, have short hikes with a great view.

Appearing in order as you drive east:

- Latourell Falls
- Shepperd's Dell
- Bridal Veil Falls
- Wahkeena Falls
- Multnomah Falls
- Oneonta Falls
- Horsetail Falls
- Elowah Falls

Note: Car break-ins along this stretch of the Columbia River Gorge are a chronic problem. If you stop to

Bridal Veil Falls

admire the waterfalls and do some of the short hikes, DO NOT leave valuables inside your car, nor leave bags that appear tempting within sight. Yes, you know there's nothing in that backpack, but thieves found a wallet in the last one they stole, so they'll take yours just to see what's inside. In addition, do not arrive, get out and put valuables, such as a purse or a pack, into your trunk and walk away. There is a history of thieves watching for this kind of activity so as to learn what you have and where it is stored. Because of its quick access to I-84, break-ins occur throughout this area, but especially in the Multnomah Falls and Oneonta Gorge parking lots. Don't start your trip with a broken window!

Bridal Veil Falls Photo © Megan Westby

Driving Directions: Continue along the Historic Columbia River Highway and stop at any of the waterfalls along the way.

☐ **Next Stop:** Latourell Falls

Introduce yourself to the waterfalls of the Columbia River Gorge with beautiful Latourell Falls. Featuring an amphitheatre with striking columnar basalt and a large yellow patch of lichen, Latourell Falls drops uninterrupted for 224 feet, often in a thin stream, before disappearing into a pool below. Follow the stairs from the parking lot up a steep but very short trail to a viewpoint above, or opt to take the near level path to the base of the falls, which leaves at the west side of the parking area, near the road.

☐ Next Stop: Shepperd's Dell Falls

Named after George Shepperd, the land owner who presented the falls and its accompanying 11 acre parcel to the City of Portland in May of 1915, Shepperd's Dell Falls drops over 90 feet in a two-tiered display before making its way under a classic 1914 deck arch bridge, a captivating example of the impressive engineering employed with the Historic Columbia River Highway. Find the beginning of the short paved path to the falls down a small flight of stairs, near the east end of the bridge.

☐ Next Stop: Bridal Veil Falls

You have your choice of two paths at Bridal Veil Falls. One leads to sweeping vistas of the Columbia River Gorge, while the other takes you to a viewing platform opposite the falls.

Make your way to the east end of the parking lot and find a trail that splits near the restrooms. The paved path to the left takes you on a short interpretive loop that leads to a collection of viewpoints high on a bluff overlooking the Columbia River. Choose the path that veers to the right, and you'll soon drop down into the forest along a gravel path that traverses a set of switchbacks, small bridges and concrete steps before leading up to a viewing platform across from Bridal Veil Falls. It's about ¼ mile, at best.

☐ **Next Stop:** Wahkeena Falls

A short 0.2 mile hike along a paved path takes you up to a historic hand-crafted stone bridge fronting Wahkeena Falls. Dropping as a fall and then a cascade for over 240 feet, it is one of the more photogenic falls you'll find in the Columbia River Gorge. Note that the bridge can become heavily ice encrusted and very treacherous when temperatures reach below freezing.

☐ **Next Stop:** Multnomah Falls

As you make your way through the list of waterfalls, you'll come upon majestic Multnomah Falls. Falling in two stages, separated by the Benson Bridge, Multnomah Falls towers at 620 feet high, making it the tallest waterfall in all of Oregon and creating such an impressive site that it draws more than 2 million visitors each year. In fact, it is the most visited natural recreation site in the Pacific Northwest.

The walk from the often busy parking area to the falls is very short, and the option exists to hike up to the Benson Bridge or to continue on all the way up to a viewing platform at the crest of the upper falls for a unique and memorable view. (1.2 Miles)

Multnomah Falls Lodge, built in 1925, offers a Visitor Center, gift shop, a snack bar, and a restaurant, which serves breakfast at 8:00 a.m., lunch at 11:00 a.m., and dinner at 4:00 p.m.

- Open: Multnomah Falls is open year-round, and the Visitor Center is open daily from 9:00 a.m. to 5:00 p.m.

Driving Directions: You'll come upon Multnomah Falls as you make your way east along the Columbia River Highway.

After visiting Multnomah Falls, you'll continue on to Oneonta Falls, Horsetail Falls and Elowah Falls. To do so, travel east from Multnomah Falls on the Historic Columbia River Scenic Byway for 3.6 miles to where you take the road to the right for *Hood River – I-84 – Route 30 East*. Take this and continue a little over 0.2 miles to where you turn right onto Frontage Road *instead of taking the onramp to I-84 Eastbound on the left*. (Note that it is OK if you do get onto I-84 here, you'll just miss Elowah Falls.) Continue on Frontage Road until you join I-84 just after passing the trailhead for Elowah Falls. Continue on I-84 East until taking *Exit 40 – Bonneville Dam*, in just under three miles.

☐ Next Stop: Oneonta Falls

A unique Columbia River Gorge adventure! In addition to offering hiking trails to Lower, Middle, and Upper Oneonta Falls, visitors may also climb over a large log jam and wade through Oneonta Creek up Oneonta Canyon to the base of Oneonta Falls! It's a popular hike, though most folks wait until the water level is low, since the water can be a tad cool!

Note: Due to the fire of 2017, all of the trails to Oneonta Falls, including through Oneonta Creek, are closed for an indefinite period of time.

☐ Next Stop: Horsetail Falls

Located right next to the Historic Columbia River Highway, graceful Horsetail Falls drops as a flowing ribbon for a full 176 feet before dispersing into a large pool at its base. Park and walk across the highway to a nearby observation area at the base of the falls. Note that the parking area on your left can come up kind of quickly, but there is a second entrance a little further along the highway.

☐ Next Stop: Elowah Falls

Plunging over a dramatic cliff face and free-falling for over 200 feet, Elowah Falls rewards those who make the easy 0.8 mile hike to its base with a captivating picturesque scene. A striking basalt amphitheatre offering scattered patches of bright yellow and green lichen forms the backdrop as the water falls and disperses below before disappearing amidst mossy boulders as McCord Creek.

Note: Due to the fire of 2017, access to the trailhead for Elowah Falls via the Historic Columbia River Highway will not be available for an indefinite period.

☐ Next Stop: Bonneville Dam Fish Viewing Window / Bonneville Lock & Dam Visitor Center

This is either a unique taste of Oregon, which provides an up close look at the salmon of the mighty Columbia River, combined with an interesting lesson on the history of the Bonneville Dam...or it's a dose of disappointment mixed with history.

A view into the fish ladder

Much of this experience depends upon if the salmon are running or not, so it's best to call the interpretive center or the Fish Count Hotline beforehand to ask if any salmon are swimming by the viewing window during the time of your visit. Fish runs in the spring, as well as late August through October, peaking in September, provide plenty of fish to see.

- See the *Average Monthly Fish Count Chart* on Page 149 to see if fish may be running during your visit.
- Bonneville Dam Interpretive Center: 541-374-8820
- Fish Count Hotline: 541-374-4011

Driving Directions: Take Exit 40 from I-84 East – Turn left at the stop and proceed under I-84 onto NE Bonneville Way. Stop at the armed security checkpoint and then proceed across the locks to the large parking lot on the east side of the interpretive center. Directions to the Fish Viewing Window are clearly displayed inside the interpretive center.

www.Discover-Oregon.com

☐ Next Stop: Bonneville Dam Hatchery

Open to the public year-round, the Bonneville Hatchery at the Bonneville Dam has display ponds holding thousands of trout and salmon fry, as well as sturgeon. Make your way to the small Sturgeon Viewing and Interpretive Center behind the hatchery building and step inside to see huge sturgeon and salmon swimming past the large viewing window. It is here that you'll see Herman, an adult White Sturgeon measuring more than 10' in length! Also, be sure to see the nearby Trout Pond, where the 18" trout are small in comparison to the others.

Bonneville Dam Hatchery
70543 NE Herman Loop
Cascade Locks, OR 97014
541-374-8393

- Exit 40 off I-84 - Located west of the Bonneville Dam

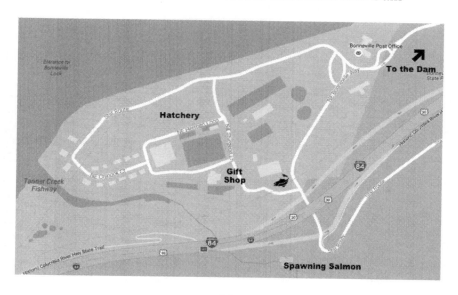

Driving Directions: Take Exit 40 from I-84 East and turn left to proceed under I-84 onto NE Bonneville Way. In a short distance, turn left onto NE Sturgeon Ln. and park near the gift shop. Then walk over to the hatchery.

If you are coming here from the Bonneville Dam Fish Viewing Window, (Page 33) look for signs to the hatchery / NE Sturgeon Ln. as you begin to leave the Dam area and approach I-84.

◻ **Next Stop:** Spawning Salmon (Sept. & Oct.)

During the last days of August, as well as the months of September and October, visitors to this area can see spawning salmon in nearby Tanner Creek.

Driving Directions: Exit I-84 at Exit 40, but instead of turning left and passing under I-84 to Bonneville Dam, turn right and park at the Wahclella Falls trailhead. (Which is an excellent 2-mile round trip triple-falls hike, by the way.) Walk over to the nearby Tanner Creek to see the salmon. Note that a parking permit, such as a Northwest Forest Pass, is required here.

www.Discover-Oregon.com

Cascade Locks, Oregon

Located in the heart of the Columbia River Gorge, the town of Cascade Locks welcomes visitors with a wealth of adventures, as well as a fascinating story that reveals the history of the indigenous people of the area and the powerful geologic, hydraulic and volcanic forces that shaped the gorge.

Driving Directions: From the Bonneville Dam area, return to I-84 Eastbound and continue east to *Exit 44 – Cascade Locks – Stevenson*. This exit rolls you right onto the main drag in town.

Note: When you leave Cascade Locks, you will travel over I-84 and take a backroad east, rejoining I-84 Eastbound at Exit 51.

☐ Cascade Locks Stop: Eastwind Drive-In

The place to hit after a day of adventure in the Columbia River Gorge, the Eastwind Drive-In offers burgers, fries, shakes and the largest chocolate & vanilla swirl soft-serve ice cream cone you'll ever see in your life! Simply continue down the main drag of Cascade Locks after getting off I-84, and you'll see it on the left.

Eastwind Drive-In
395 NW Wa Na Pa Street
Cascade Locks, OR 97014
541-374-8380

www.Discover-Oregon.com

☐ **Cascade Locks Stop:** Historical Museum

Built in 1905, the museum provides guests with a look at the history of the Cascade Locks area through displays, photos and artifacts. Outside, in its own climate controlled building, is The Oregon Pony, the first steam locomotive ever used in Oregon.

> Cascade Locks Historical Museum
> SW Portage Rd.
> Cascade Locks, OR 97014
> 541-374-8535

- Open May – September - 12:00 p.m. – 5:00 p.m. - $3
- Closed Mondays, except holidays

Driving Directions: Heading east, take the first left after the Eastwind Drive-In onto SW Portage Road and follow this to the Port of Cascade Locks Marine Park. Take the first left after passing underneath the railroad tracks.

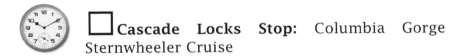

☐ **Cascade Locks Stop:** Columbia Gorge Sternwheeler Cruise

See the Columbia River Gorge from "the best view on the Columbia" during a one or two hour sightseeing and interpretive cruise aboard the historic Columbia Gorge Sternwheeler. Approximately three cruises per day in the summer. Call 503-224-3900 to book your cruise.

Columbia Gorge Sternwheeler
299 SW Portage Rd.
Cascade Locks, OR 97014
541-374-8427

Driving Directions: From the Historical Museum, drive back east along SW Portage Road to the 4-way intersection by the railroad tracks, but instead of turning right to pass back underneath the tracks, proceed straight. Drive 1/8 mile to the Visitor Center and Locks Waterfront Café, located in the Cascade Locks Marine Park. Note that the Locks Waterfront Café here is open from 10:30 a.m. – 6:00 p.m. daily, May to October. 541-645-0372

■**Cascade Locks Stop:** Sacagawea Bronze Statue

See this beautiful larger-than-life bronze statue of Sacagawea (Sah-cog-a-way) located outside the Visitor Center and Locks Waterfront Cafe at 299 SW Portage Rd., Cascade Locks.

To Leave Cascade Locks

If you're proceeding to Hood River from Cascade Locks:

- Drive east on Wa Na Pa Street through Cascade Locks
- Veer left onto Forest Ln.
- Follow this until it passes over I-84 and then proceed left / east on Frontage Rd.
- Turn right onto Herman Creek Rd. / Wyeth Rd. Note: This is not the turnoff for the nearby Herman Creek Trailhead, which occurs at .37 miles, though both roads have the same "Herman Creek Rd." name.
- Turn left at 3.6 miles and then turn right onto I-84 Eastbound
- Follow I-84 to Hood River and take Exit 63.

If you're driving directly to Hood River without stopping in Cascade Locks:

- Follow I-84 to Hood River and take Exit 63.

If you're not stopping in Hood River:

- If you're not stopping in Hood River, then continue to Exit 69 for Mosier, OR and Hwy 30.

☐ Next *Look*: Historic Broughton Flume

As you begin to approach Hood River on I-84, you'll see a large freeway sign on the right that reads *Exit 58 – Mitchell Point Overlook*. Do not take this exit, but at this point, while you're driving, look directly ahead to the opposite shore of the Columbia River and you'll spot a gray horizontal ribbon of old timbers and planks crossing a field of rocks just above the river. These boards are the remains of the historic Broughton Flume, a raised wooden flume, or channel of water, which carried rough-cut lumber from a sawmill in Willard, WA to the Broughton Mill at Hood, WA, on the bank of the Columbia River. Long since abandoned, it is slowly decaying at the hands of time.

Photo courtesy of the History Museum of Hood River County.

Hood River, Oregon

Home to a busy downtown area filled with recreation-minded folks, the town of Hood River is a launching point for countless outdoor adventures on the eastern end of the Columbia River Gorge National Scenic Area.

You'll find Hood River at Exit 63 on I-84.

 □ **Hood River Stop:** Western Antique Aeroplane & Automobile Museum (WAAAM)

 One of the largest collections of flight-ready antique aeroplanes, along with over 175 intricately restored automobiles from the 1910s through 1950s, can be found under two large hangars spanning over 3.5 acres. In addition, visitors will find antique tractors, motorcycles, military vehicles, toys and more.

Western Antique Aeroplane & Automobile Museum
1600 Air Museum Rd.
Hood River, OR 97031
541-308-1600

- Open Daily 9:00 a.m. – 5:00 p.m. – Closed Thanksgiving Day, Christmas Day and New Years Day
- Adults: $16, Seniors & Veterans: $14, Kids 5 – 18: $7

Driving Directions: Take Exit 63 from I-84 and turn right / south onto N 2nd Street. Follow this for 0.1 miles to Oak Street. From the corner of Oak Street and North 2nd Street, turn right and proceed west on Oak Street for 0.6 miles to 13th Street. Turn left onto 13th Street and proceed 0.7 miles to where 13th Street becomes 12th Street. Continue south another 2.2 miles as 12th Street becomes Tucker Road, making a couple of 90 degree turns before reaching Air Museum Road and the Western Antique Aeroplane & Automobile Museum.

☐ Hood River Stop: Watch World-Class Kiteboarders and Sailboarders

Hood River is one of the two best places in the world for kiteboarding and sailboarding, with the other being Hawaii. Visit the "Event Site" to park, get out and watch all of the action up close.

Driving Directions: From the WAAAM, return to the corner of Oak Street and North 2nd Street in Hood River. From here, proceed north on North 2nd Street as it crosses over I-84 and works its way down to the Event Site at the 0.4 mile mark.

☐ Next Stop: Mosier, OR - Mosier Twin Tunnels

Closed to motorized traffic, the paved Historic Columbia River Highway State Trail takes visitors along the old Columbia River Highway to the Mosier Twin Tunnels, two impressive tunnels blasted into the basalt cliffside nearly 100 years ago. Inspired by the design of the Axenstrasse on Lake Lucerne, Switzerland, the tunnels were built with large viewing portals and observation walkways offering travelers a unique view of the gorge. Of note is the inscription carved into the rock on the north side wall at the east end of the tunnels.

It reads...

Snowbound
November 19 to 27, 1921
Chas J. Sadilek
E. B Marvin

Driving Directions: From the Event Site, return to I-84 on North 2nd Street and take the onramp to I-84 Eastbound. Proceed east on I-84 and take Exit 69 for Mosier, OR and Hwy 30. Turn right onto Hwy 30 / Historic Columbia River Highway Scenic Byway at the exit. At 0.15 miles, turn left / north onto Rock Creek Rd. and follow this 0.6 miles west to the paved parking area on the left. Park, pay the parking fee, and then hike back down the road a short distance to the trailhead. Hike from here on the paved road 0.8 miles to the old Mosier Tunnels and viewpoint. The road is closed to cars, but open to cyclists and pedestrians, so be sure to stay to the right as you walk.

Note: While driving from Hood River to Mosier on I-84, you can spot the west entrance to the Mosier Tunnels, as well as some of the viewing windows, up on the cliffside immediately after passing the freeway sign that reads *Exit 69 - Mosier 1 Mile.*

☐ **Next Stop:** Rowena Crest Viewpoint

This "must stop" location gives travelers a commanding view of the east end of the Columbia River Gorge, a walk among plateaus covered in wildflowers, and a high vantage point over the picturesque Rowena Loops of the old Columbia River Highway.

Driving Directions: From the Mosier Twin Tunnels trailhead, drive back east the way you came and continue on the Historic Columbia River Scenic Byway / Hwy 30 *through* Mosier. *Do not return to I-84 Eastbound here.* From Mosier, continue on the Historic Columbia River Highway Scenic Byway / Hwy 30 east for 6.6 scenic miles to Rowena Crest.

The Dalles, Oregon

Your next set of stops are in The Dalles, which showcases the ancient, rich and dramatic history of the eastern end of the Columbia River Gorge, as reflected in its archaeological sites, historical buildings, ornate Victorian and Gothic style homes, and fine museums.

☐ The Dalles Stop: Columbia Gorge Discovery Center & Museum

At over 48,000 square feet, the Columbia Gorge Discovery Center & Wasco County Historical Museum showcases a vast array of exhibits which explain the many wonders of this area, including the forces that shaped the Columbia River Gorge, the 10,000 year old culture of the gorge's native inhabitants, the journey of Lewis & Clark, modern day history and much more.

Columbia Gorge Discovery Center & Museum
5000 Discovery Drive
The Dalles, OR 97058
541-296-8600

- Admission: $9.00 – Ages 6 – 16: $5.00
- Open Daily: 9:00 a.m. – 5:00 p.m.

Driving Directions: From the Rowena Crest Viewpoint, continue down into the Rowena Loops and proceed on the Historic Columbia River Highway Scenic Byway / Highway 30 east towards The Dalles. At 7.0 miles from Rowena Crest, turn left / east onto Discovery Drive, which leads you under I-84 and back north to the Columbia Gorge Discovery Center & Museum.

☐ The Dalles Stop: Klindt's Booksellers

The next chapter of your trip takes you to Klindt's Booksellers, the oldest bookstore in Oregon. Selling books since 1870, and from this bookstore since 1893, its shelves offer an abundance of books, including an impressive collection of new books every month. You can even find our Oregon Road Trip books here!

Klindt's Booksellers
315 E. 2nd Street
The Dalles, OR 97058
541-296-3355

- Open Monday – Saturday: 8:00 a.m. – 6:00 p.m.
- Sunday: 11:00 a.m. – 4:00 p.m.

Driving Directions: From the Discovery Center, continue east on the Historic Columbia River Highway Scenic Byway / Highway 30 into The Dalles and stay on Hwy 30 as it automatically turns into W 6th St. (Continue straight – Do not turn left onto Webber St.) Continue on W 6th St. as it veers leftward onto W 3rd Place before joining E. 3rd Street. Follow this and then turn left / north onto Federal St. Park in street parking spots just across E. 2nd Street and walk west to Klindt's Booksellers.

☐ **The Dalles Stop:** City of The Dalles Fire Museum

This free self-guided museum offers a unique taste of Oregon history with its two old-fashioned steam-powered fire engines from the 1800s, as well as an interesting collection of antique fire-fighting equipment, artifacts and photos.

City of The Dalles Fire Museum
313 Court Street
The Dalles, OR 97058
541-296-5481 - xt 1119

- Located inside the City Hall
- Closed on Weekends
- Open Monday – Friday 8:00 a.m. – 5:00 p.m.

Walking Directions: From Klindt's, walk west on E 2nd Street for 1.5 blocks to Court Street. Turn left / south and walk 1 block to the City Hall building at 313 Court Street. Walk in the front door, through the hallway, and down the stairs to the small museum in the back.

☐ **The Dalles Stop:** National Neon Sign Museum

Located in the stately 1910 Elks Lodge in The Dalles is the National Neon Sign Museum. Here, you'll find a growing collection of colorful signs from the past, many of which you may recognize, and all arranged with interpretive displays that walk visitors through the chronological history of store front advertising, beginning with simple reflective signs in the mid-19th century before progressing to signs lit by the new incandescent light bulb in the late 1800s, and colorful neon then following in 1910.

Be sure to make your way upstairs to walk among a collection of creative storefront facades, including Verne's Television Repair, Peggy's Beauty Shop, Chapman's Ice Cream, Medich's Steaks & Chicken & BBQ diner, and, of course, Frank Neon Sign Co., all attracting customers with their colorful neon signs.

National Neon Sign Museum
200 East 3rd Street
The Dalles, OR 97058

- Open: Thursday through Saturday – 10:00 a.m. to 5:00 p.m.

Walking Directions: From The Dalles Fire Museum, walk to the National Neon Sign Museum, which is just across the street, on the opposite corner.

☐ The Dalles Stop: Fort Dalles Museum and Anderson Homestead

Dating back to 1905, the impressive Fort Dalles Museum is one of Oregon's two oldest history museums. Here you'll wander through a collection of original buildings from the 1856 Fort Dalles military compound, each offering a themed display of rare  artifacts and items reflecting the amazing history of the area and its early pioneers. In addition, you'll find a barn filled with over 30 antique horse-drawn wagons and automobiles.

500 West 15th and Garrison
The Dalles, OR 97058
541-296-4547

- Admission: $8 - Students Ages 7 - 17: $1.00
- Open Monday - Sunday: 10:00 a.m. - 5:00 p.m. - March through November.
- Closed December, January and February.

Driving Directions: Head back to your car and, from Klindt's Booksellers, drive west on E 2nd Street for 2.5 blocks to Union Street. Turn left / south onto Union Street and proceed for 0.6 miles to E 14th Street. Turn right / west here and follow this for 4 blocks to Garrison Street. Turn left here and continue one block to the museum.

☐ The Dalles Stop: Rorick House Museum

At over 165 years old, the small Malcolm A. Moody House, home of the Rorick House Museum, is the oldest remaining house in The Dalles.

The Rorick House Museum
300 W 13th St.
The Dalles, OR 97058

- Open only during the summer months

Driving Directions: From the Fort Dalles Museum, drive north on Garrison Street for 2 blocks to W 13th Street. Turn right here and continue two blocks to the Rorick House on your right.

☐ **Next Stop:** Historic Petersburg School

A well-preserved historic one room school house, which served students in The Dalles area. Note that it is not open to the public.

Historic Petersburg School
15 Mile Road
The Dalles, OR 97014

Driving Directions: Return to W 3rd Street / Hwy 30 in The Dalles and proceed east. Just before the exit for Hwy 197 South, follow the signs for SE Frontage Road and veer left onto SE Frontage Road / State Road through a kind of funky small interchange. (You're now passing Big Jim's Drive-In on your right, which is a great place to eat!) Continue east on SE Frontage Road / State Road and follow this as it turns into Fifteen Mile Road. At 3.2 miles, turn left / northeast onto what is still Fifteen Mile Road. (It's going to seem like Fifteen Mile Road continues straight, but that's now 8 Mile Road.) Drive 0.3 miles and find the school on the left.

Note: The Historic Petersburg School House is a popular starting point for many outstanding cycling routes in this area, all of which head south and east of the school. For an excellent book of cycling routes in Oregon, we highly recommend *75 Classic Rides Oregon: The Best Road Biking Routes* by Jim Moore.

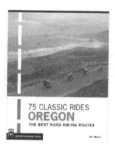

A Whimsical Detour

Want to see a rafter (flock) of wild turkeys? Perhaps anywhere from 20 to 100 of them? Then leave the Petersburg School and return west on 15 Mile Road for 0.3 miles. Turn left / south onto 8 Mile road and immediately begin looking for wild turkeys in the field to your right, usually close to the tree line. If you don't see them here, continue driving a little further south on 8 Mile road, all the while looking for turkeys. You are most likely to see them within the first two miles after your turn. If you are unsuccessful, you may continue driving south on 8 Mile road, where you may spot a different rafter of wild turkeys on either side of the road anytime prior to reaching the five mile mark. Once finished, return to the Petersburg School and continue your road trip east.

☐ Next Stop: Pathfinders Memorial

High on a road bank, clearly out of place among the wheat fields of the area, stands like a sentinel a single column of basalt. Affixed to its side is a bronze plaque, which reads... *Here lie many pathfinders to the Oregon country – Erected by The Wasco County Pioneer*

Association 1935. This memorial is dedicated to those Oregon Trail pioneers who lost their lives and were buried in a burial ground adjacent to a nearby campsite used by early pioneers on their way to Fort Dalles in The Dalles.

Driving Directions: From the Historic Petersburg School House, continue east on Fifteen Mile Road for 6.7 miles. You'll spot the lone basalt column up on the bank to the left, just to the side of the road.

TONIGHT'S LODGING THE BALCH HOTEL - DUFUR, OR

The historic 1907 Balch Hotel is a highlight of the trip. Josiah and Claire welcome you with homemade cookies, a refreshing drink, and a slower, genuinely friendly pace before directing you to your well-appointed period-specific room.

In addition to being your first night's stay, the award-winning Balch Hotel is also a fun weekend destination, with a lot of events occurring here throughout the year. Be sure to sign up for their email newsletter to stay in the know.

If your travel timing works out, we highly recommend you dine at the Balch Hotel this evening. Find a table under the string lights on the patio and enjoy the cool evening as you watch the sun set behind Mt. Hood.

Historic Balch Hotel
40 Heimrich St.
Dufur, OR 97021
541-467-2277
www.BalchHotel.com

- Check in between 3:00 p.m. and 9:00 p.m.
- Dinner and a "delicious house made breakfast" are available – Dining reservations are required
- To-Go breakfasts are also available with advance notice
- Ask for a room with a Mt. Hood view
- Stock up for the next day's journey at Kramer's Market in downtown Dufur
- The Balch Hotel does not accommodate pets

Note: If it's warm out, then be sure to explore the landscaped grounds, complete with outdoor seating, soft shaded grass, a small pond and a patio.

If you visit Kramer's Market, be sure to walk across the street and look in the windows to see a unique Oregon sight!

Driving directions to the Balch Hotel from the Pathfinders Memorial:

From the Pathfinders Memorial, continue on Fifteen Mile Road for 3.9 miles to Kelly Cutoff Road. Turn right / west onto Kelly Cutoff Road and follow this for 2.5 miles, where you'll then turn left / south onto Emerson Loop Road. From here, proceed 5.5 miles to Ward Road. Turn left / south onto Ward Rd. and follow this 3.4 miles to Hwy 197. Turn left / south onto Hwy 197 and drive 4 miles to Dufur, OR. Take the exit to Dufur and follow the main road into the heart of town. You'll find the Historic Balch Hotel on your left at 40 Heimrich St.

Lodging Option: Victor Trevitt Guest House

Built in 1868 and recently restored with impeccable period-specific detail and antique furnishings, the historic Victor Trevitt Guest House makes for a nice alternative if the Balch Hotel is full.

The house will accommodate up to 4 guests, with 2 bedrooms, 3 beds and 1.5 baths.

Your hosts, Alan and Bev Eagy, live right next door in the historic 1867 Ben Snipes house, to the west.

Note that the Victor Trevitt Guest House is located in The Dalles, 14 miles north of Dufur.

Victor Trevitt Guest House
214 W 4th Street
The Dalles, OR
541-980-3522

Born in 1827, Victor Trevitt moved to The Dalles in 1853, and as a printer, entrepreneur, businessman, state legislator and the first judge to preside at the small Wasco County Courthouse, he played an important role in shaping the growth of this area and developing The Dalles.

www.Discover-Oregon.com

Notes

DAY TWO

DUFUR TO CONDON

"We have good roads comparatively. We mean good roads if the sloughs are not belly deep and the hills not right straight up and down and not rock enough to turn the wagon over."

Henry Allyn - August 11, 1852

DAY 2
DUFUR TO CONDON

Day 2 – Date: /   /

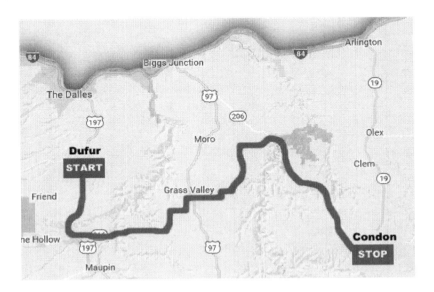

Summary: Where You're Going Today

- Dufur
- Tygh Valley
- Grass Valley
- Cottonwood Canyon State Park
- Condon

With today's route you begin to journey into eastern Oregon, driving into open vistas of rolling wheat fields dotted with towering white windmills spinning majestically into the distance.

Tonight's Lodging:

- The Hotel Condon

Today's Mileage: 100 Miles

Reservations Needed for This Segment:

- The Hotel Condon - 541-384-4624

Before You Leave:

 Fill your gas tank in Dufur or in Tygh Valley, which is your first stop of the day. By the way, this small gas pump icon, which you'll see throughout the book, is the actual gas pump found in Frenchglen, Oregon.

Start

Enjoy a late start on your second day and spend a little more time at each stop along your route, as today's journey is somewhat short compared to Day 3. Linger over your breakfast at the Balch Hotel, walk through the Dufur Historical Museum just up the street, stroll through town and take in the view of Mt. Hood, and when you're finished, hit the road, where you'll explore northern Central Oregon before making your way to the beautifully restored historic Hotel Condon.

 As an option to having breakfast at the Balch Hotel, you may also want to consider Molly B's Diner in Tygh Valley. *Bring cash, as they do not accept credit cards.*

☐ First Stop: Dufur Living History Museum

Before leaving Dufur, walk one block north from The Balch Hotel to the Dufur Living History Museum. Here, you can stroll among antique harvesting equipment, hay wagons, buckboards, an old blacksmith shop and more on the grounds outside before stepping into one of the original buildings on the site dating back to the turn of the 20th century. Inside, you'll find many impressive exhibits and displays that depict life in Oregon and the Pacific Northwest during the late 1800s to early 1900s. While you're there, be sure to ask about the story behind the bell atop the old Endersby School! The museum is free, but donations are gladly accepted.

Dufur Living History Museum
40 Main Street
Dufur, OR 97021
541-467-2205

- Open: Wednesday through Saturday – 10:00 a.m. to 5:00 p.m.

☐ Next Stop: Kramer's Market

After visiting the Dufur Living History Museum, walk over to Kramer's Market, which has been the center of Dufur for over 100 years, since 1905. Inside this old-fashioned store, you'll find a busy marketplace offering all kinds of goods, as well as local wines, a restaurant and deli, the world famous "Kramer's Sausage", and picnic tables inside and out at which to enjoy your meal. This is an excellent place to stop if you are cycling, fishing, climbing or hiking out in this part of Oregon. After you visit Kramer's, make sure you walk directly across the street to peek into the storefront windows. We won't spoil the surprise.

Kramer's Market
121 N Main Street
Dufur, OR 97021
541-467-2455

- Open: Monday through Saturday – 7:00 a.m. to 7:00 p.m., Sunday 9:00 a.m. to 5:00 p.m.

☐ Next Stop: Tygh Valley, OR

Visit the small town of Tygh Valley before continuing east on today's journey.

Driving Directions: Leave Dufur, OR and drive south on Hwy 197 approximately 17 miles, where you can take a right onto Tygh Valley Road, which leads to Tygh Valley, OR.

☐ Next Stop: White River Falls State Park

A small sign and dirt road off Hwy 216 lead to an overlooked Oregon gem you don't want to miss.

Driving Directions: After leaving Tygh Valley, drive east on Hwy 216 / Shears Bridge Highway for approximately four miles until you see a small sign on your right which leads to White River Falls State Park.

☐ **Next Stop**: Oregon Raceway Park

Just two miles east of Grass Valley, OR sits the Oregon Raceway Park, a 2.3 mile paved road course located amidst the wheat fields of eastern Oregon. You're more than welcome to stop in and watch any race events, and there is no fee for doing so. If the park is open

and an event is not occurring, you're also welcome to receive a free tour of the track. You'll board a van and make four laps around the course, all while learning about the facility. Reservations are not required, but it is a good idea to call first to see if the track is open on the day you are passing by.

Oregon Raceway Park
93811 Blagg Lane
Grass Valley, OR 97029
541-531-5695
541-333-2452 (Track Office)

- Mon. – Fri. 9:00 a.m. – 5:00 p.m. – Closed for lunch 12:00 p.m. – 1:00 p.m.

Driving Directions: Continue east on Hwy 216 from Tygh Valley for 29 miles until you turn left onto Hwy 97 North, just south of the town of Grass Valley. Continue approximately 1/2 mile into Grass Valley on Hwy 97 and turn right / east onto North Street, which turns into Blagg Lane. Follow this out to the Oregon Raceway Park, which you'll find on your left 2 miles from Grass Valley.

wwwDiscover-Oregon.com

☐ **Next Stop**: Cottonwood Canyon State Park

 As Oregon's second largest State Park, 8,000 acre Cottonwood Canyon State Park is set in a scenic rugged landscape carved by the mighty John Day River.

The park offers interesting interpretive displays which convey the ranching history of the area, complete with an old barn and windmill. A short interpretive trail leading from the main parking area offers an excellent overview of the park.

Note: Camping with water and bathroom facilities is available here.

Driving Directions: From the Oregon Raceway Park, continue east on Blagg Lane until it curves north and reaches Smith-Todd Rd. at 3.8 miles. Turn right onto Smith Todd Rd. and follow this 1 mile to Lone Rock Road. Turn left / north onto Lone Rock Rd. and then turn right at 2 miles onto Hart Rd. (It's a small sign for Hart Rd.) - Continue left / north on Hart Rd. when it meets Higley Loop - Continue on Hart Rd. as it turns into Hay Canyon Rd. - Then turn right onto Monkland Ln., which travels east and connects to Hwy 206 - Turn right onto Hwy 206 and follow this east to Cottonwood Canyon State Park.

☐ Next Stop: Old Homestead

As you travel east along Hwy 206, you'll pass a decrepit white house sitting alone in a wheat field. It's tempting to stop and walk through it, but the interior is covered with graffiti, the walls are filled with holes, and the flooring is unsafe. In addition,  rattlesnakes like to hide in the old boards out back. (Photo) This is an interesting site which is best enjoyed from the road.

☐ Next Stop: Windmills

Your Discover Oregon journey is all about exploring and experiencing Oregon. It may be convenient to observe the towering windmills in this area through your windshield as you drive past, but this is your opportunity to stop, get out  and get an up close look at their massive blades as they cut through the air with a roar.

"You know, it'd be a lot less windy out here if they'd turn off these big fans." - Tim Thiessen

☐ Next Stop: Condon, OR

To achieve a balance with tomorrow's journey, today is a somewhat shorter day, which is perfect for walking through Condon and exploring its quaint shops or just enjoying the book you brought along. You didn't bring one? Then stop in at Powell's Bookstore and buy the perfect book for your trip.

Yes, Condon is home to a small Powell's Bookstore!

Today's journey ends at the historic Hotel Condon.

Driving Directions: From Cottonwood Canyon State Park, continue east on Hwy 206 until you reach Condon, OR.

☐ Condon Stop: The Drive-In

Condon offers a few places for lunch and dinner, including the Round-up Café, Condon Café, the lunch counter at Country Flowers, and the Hotel Condon. In addition, you'll find The Drive-In, an old school "burger joint" at the south end of town offering fine fare served by nice folks.

The Drive-In
433 S. Main Street
Condon, OR 97823
541-384-3922

- Open Monday – Sunday – 11:00 a.m. – 7:00 p.m.
- Closed Sundays over the winter

☐ Condon Stop: Powell's Bookstore

Michael Powell, the Founder of the world famous Powell's Bookstore in Portland, also has a small shop in Condon. Better yet, they carry our books!

201 South Main Street
Condon, OR 97823
541-384-4120

- Located inside the Country Flowers store
- Unique and unusual quality gifts, Powell's Bookstore, soda fountain and a lunch counter

☐ Condon Stop: Gilliam County Historical Museum

Just northwest of town, off of Hwy 19, you'll find the Gilliam County Historical Museum. Here, visitors will find a collection of historical buildings, including an 1884 hand-hewn log cabin, a 1900 school house, and a early 1900s barber shop, all  furnished with period-specific furnishings, photos and artifacts reflecting the lives and culture of the early pioneers of the area. Admission is free, but donations are welcome.

Highway 19
Condon, OR 97823
541-384-4233

- Open Wednesday – Sunday – 1:00 p.m. – 5:00 p.m.
- Open May 1st through October 31st

TONIGHT'S LODGING HOTEL CONDON - CONDON, OR

The beautiful Hotel Condon is a taste of Oregon history in a peaceful small town setting. Built in 1920 and impeccably renovated in 2001, its luxurious guest rooms and suites welcome travelers with modern-day amenities and services.

Hotel Condon
202 South Main Street
Condon, OR 97823
541-384-4624
www.HotelCondon.com

Day Three

Blue Mountain
Oregon Scenic Byway

Condon to Baker City

August Bohne – Circa 1907

DAY 3
CONDON TO BAKER CITY

Day 3 – Date: /   /

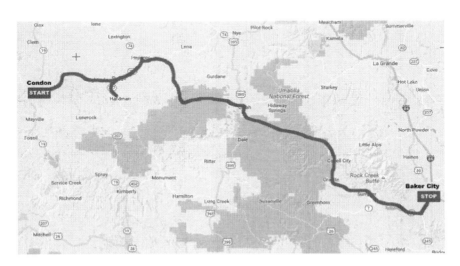

Summary: Where You're Going Today

- Condon
- Heppner
- Ukiah
- Granite
- Baker City

Tonight's Lodging:

- The Geiser Grand Hotel *or*
- The Wisdom House

Today's route takes connects you with the Blue Mountain Oregon Scenic Byway, where you'll transition from open vistas of rolling wheat fields to forested terrain, all while experiencing more of Oregon's history.

Rising to 5,296' in elevation between Heppner and Ukiah, the byway is open from early to mid-may, when the snow melts, through the summer months and into October, when winter returns. Be sure to carry a small shovel with you if you are traveling early or late in the season, as it will be invaluable should you become stuck in any snow.

Note: During the winter, the byway is not plowed, and it is closed to car traffic due to deep snow.

For the latest road conditions in this area, contact the Heppner Ranger District:

> 117 S Main Street
> Heppner, OR 97836
> 541-676-9187

Be sure to fill your gas tank in Condon, OR before leaving, as reliable options for gas are extremely limited between Heppner and Baker City. Gas may or may not be available in Ukiah, as it depends upon if the small market there (located on the left as you arrive into town from the northwest) is open during the time of year you arrive, as well as the time of day.

Today's Mileage: 200 Miles

Reservations Needed for This Segment:

- Geiser Grand Hotel, Baker City, OR – 541-523-1889 – Make reservations for 2 nights (Days 3 & 4)
    or
- Wisdom House, Baker City, OR – VRBO #: 726034 – Make reservations for 2 nights (Days 3 & 4)

Start

Travel east on Hwy 206 from Condon to the town of Heppner. Here you'll connect with the Blue Mountain Scenic Byway as it travels southeast, climbing into high-altitude forests and mountain meadows, discovering Ukiah and Granite along the way before finishing your day at historic Baker City.

Driving Directions: Depart Condon, OR and drive east on Hwy 206 towards Heppner.

☐ First Stop: Ruggs, OR / Hardman, OR

Take a short detour south to visit the small ghost town of Hardman, OR before continuing east.

First settled in the 1870s, the town that would eventually become known as Hardman at one time was the center of activity for this area, complete with three general stores, two hotels, a barber shop, post office, telephone office, a church and even a skating rink. Today, only a few structures remain, with the others being lost to the elements of time.

Driving Directions: From Condon, drive east on Hwy 206 to immediately before the small town of Ruggs, which consists of a quaint home and some tall concrete silos. At Ruggs, take a detour from today's journey and turn right / south onto Hwy 207 and follow this 8.6 miles to Hardman.

Return to Route:

To resume your Discover Oregon journey to Heppner, OR, retrace your steps back to Ruggs, OR and then continue east on Hwy 206 until you reach Heppner, where you'll intersect with the Blue Mountain Scenic Byway.

☐ Next Stop: Heppner, OR

Incorporated in 1887, historic Heppner, Oregon is known as the "Gateway to the Blue Mountains." Welcoming visitors throughout the year with a mix of events, including the Morrow County Fair, Oregon Trail Pro-Rodeo, the "Wee Bit O'Ireland" and July 4th Blues Festival, Heppner offers something for everyone, all while showcasing an abundance of outdoor activities ranging from fishing, camping and hiking, to snowmobiling, snowshoeing and cross-country skiing.

 Note: You'll want to top off your gas tank in Heppner.

☐ Heppner Stop: Morrow County Museum

One of the finest collections of pioneer, agricultural, and homestead history in the northwest.

Morrow County Museum
444 N. Main Street
Heppner, OR 97836
541-676-5524

- Open May 1st thru September
- Tuesday – Friday 1:00 p.m. – 5:00 p.m., Sat. 11:00 a.m. – 3:00 p.m.
- Donations are welcomed

www.Discover-Oregon.com

☐ **Heppner Stop:** Morrow County Agriculture Museum

A large museum dedicated to the practices of Farming, Ranching and Forestry.

Morrow County Agricultural
Museum
444 N. Main Street
Heppner, OR 97836
541-676-5524

- Open May 1st through September
- Friday: 1:00 p.m. – 5:00 p.m., Saturday: 11:00 a.m. to 3:00 p.m.
- Donations are welcomed

Note that the Morrow County Museum and the Morrow County Agricultural Museum are both all volunteer operations. If you would like to see the museums, but you won't be in Heppner during their operating hours, then feel free to call 24 hours in advance to arrange to have a volunteer come by and let you in. They are more than happy to do so. You will also find phone numbers posted on the front doors of the museums.

☐ **Next Stop:** Ukiah, OR

Unfortunately, there currently isn't a lot to see in Ukiah, OR. As such, there aren't any stops or points of interest listed here.

If need be, you can get 87 octane gas in Ukiah, if the small market there is open.

Continue on the Blue Mountain Scenic Byway south out of town towards Granite, OR.

<u>Driving Directions:</u>

From Heppner, OR to Ukiah, OR (Approx. 45 Miles)

Begin by heading back the way you came into Heppner, backtracking south on Hwy 206 for approximately one mile. Turn left / east onto Willow Creek Road / NF 053 – At 22.5 miles Willow Creek Rd. turns into Western Raite Ln. / NF-053 – (Note: "P Willow Creek Rd." turns right / south at this point, but do not take this road) Follow Western Raite Ln. to Ukiah – Note: 1 Mile west of Ukiah, you will cross Hwy 395 and continue on Hwy 244 East, which leads directly into Ukiah, OR.

Continuing: Ukiah, OR to Granite, OR – To Baker City

Upon leaving Ukiah, you will drive SE and climb into the forest again, passing through the expansive Bridge Creek Wildlife Area, home to the wintering grounds of over 1,000 Rocky Mountain elk, one of the largest herds of its kind in the nation. Look for elk and Mule Deer along the entire route, especially in the mountain meadows.

Along this route, you'll find the North Fork John Day Overlook Interpretive Site, offering a spectacular view of the North Fork John Day Wilderness to the immediate south, the Strawberry Mountain Wilderness to the far south, and the Bridge Creek Wildlife Area to the west.

Due to snow in the higher elevations, the scenic byway from Ukiah towards Granite is open only from mid-may to October. It climbs to double summits of 5,549' at 15.7 miles from Ukiah, and again to 5,658' at 32.2 miles.

Note: During the winter, the byway is closed to car traffic due to deep snow. It is not plowed and you cannot drive between Ukiah and Granite.

For the latest road conditions, contact:

- The Ukiah Ranger Station - 541-427-5308.
- The Wallowa Whitman Ranger Station – 541-523-6391

Driving Directions:

At Ukiah, turn right / south onto Camas St., which turns into Soap Hill Rd / NF-052. Take NF-052 south out of town to NFD 73, which you'll merge with at 40.8 miles. (Note: There is a junction at approximately 1.5 miles north of where you merge with NFD 73. Go right / south here, as the road heading south is still NF-052 until it merges with NFD 73) Upon reaching NFD 73, follow this south towards Granite, OR. At this point, you will have now left the Blue Mountain Scenic Byway and be on the Elkhorn Scenic Byway. Follow this south past Granite, OR and Sumpter, OR until you reach Hwy 7. Turn left onto Hwy 7 and follow this east to Baker City.

Note: Do not stop at Granite, OR or Sumpter, OR today, as you will visit these towns in two days as you travel the Elkhorn Scenic Byway clockwise north to Anthony Lakes, Haines and then to Union, OR.

Note: There is premium 91 octane gas available in Granite, OR, provided the small market / lodge there is open.

TONIGHT'S LODGING
GEISER GRAND HOTEL -
BAKER CITY, OR

Built in 1889, but recently restored in period-specific detail, the elegant Victorian era Geiser Grand Hotel features the largest stained glass ceiling in the Northwest and welcomes guests into the heart of downtown Baker City, Oregon.

You'll find the hotel on the right as you make your way north on Main Street into Baker City. Look for the large tower cupola and turn east onto Washington Avenue to find parking available in the lot behind the hotel.

Note: You will be making reservations for *two* nights.

Geiser Grand Historic Hotel
1996 Main St.
Baker City, OR 97814
541-523-1889 / 888-434-7374

☐ Lodging Option: The Wisdom House

For another taste of historical Oregon, consider staying at the Wisdom House, home of the first Pharmacist in Baker City, John W. Wisdom. Built in 1878, this Gothic and Italianate style home is the oldest in Baker City and is conveniently located only two blocks off Main Street. With its impressive restoration and beautifully restored interior containing upscale features and amenities, we highly recommend it for your stay in Baker City, provided it is available. Visit its VRBO page at vrbo.com/726034.

- Wisdom House
- WisdomHouse@TheGeo.net
- HistoricWisdomHouse.com

Notes

DAY FOUR

EXPLORE BAKER CITY

"I will say that this part of Oregon is the most fertile for rocks and sagebrush of any part of the world I have ever seen."

Charlotte Stearns Pengra - August 22, 1853

DAY 4
EXPLORE BAKER CITY

Day 4 – Date: /   /

Today involves very little driving. Instead, you'll stay closer to home as you explore the history, architecture and flavor of Baker City, Oregon.

☐ **Breakfast:** Lone Pine Cafe

Serving breakfast and lunch, the Lone Pine Café is a quaint café offering excellent fare. It's located a couple of blocks south of the Geiser Grand Hotel and makes for an excellent way to start your day. Outdoor, window and table seating are all available.

The Lone Pine Cafe
1825 Main St.
Baker City, OR 97814
541-523-1805

☐ **Next Stop:** Geiser Grand Hotel "Basement Museum"

Visit the small museum in the "basement" of the Geiser Grand Hotel and discover, among other things, why the main street of Baker City, and most small towns throughout eastern Oregon and the west, are so wide.

☐ **Next Stop:** Historic Walking Tour

Baker City is home to more than 100 structures on the National Register of Historic Buildings. In fact, there are nine historic buildings and Victorian era homes with very interesting architecture within eight blocks of the Geiser Grand Hotel, so much can be discovered simply by walking through the nearby neighborhoods. A walking tour map is available in town or via a PDF download online.

☐ **Next Stop:** Leo Adler House Museum

Built in 1889, the museum showcases the carefully restored Italianate home of Leo Adler, whom built a $21 million dollar fortune through the sale of newspapers and magazines at a time when they were a very important form of news and entertainment. Guided tours walk visitors through the home room by room while telling the amazing story of Mr. Adler.

Note: The purchase of a ticket to the Leo Adler House Museum entitles you to a discount on the price of a ticket for the nearby Baker Heritage Museum.

Leo Adler House Museum
2305 Main St.
Baker City, OR 97814
541-523-7913

- Open Memorial Day to Labor Day. Fri., Sat., Sun. and Monday – 10:00 a.m. – 3:30 p.m. Hours can vary, so it is best to call ahead to confirm if the home will be open.
- Admission: $6.00.

☐ Next Stop: Baker Heritage Museum

An interesting and well-curated museum displays the history of Baker County. A myriad exhibits showcase the history and importance of mining, timber harvesting, ranching and farming in this area, as well as the lives of those who lived in the region throughout the years.

Note: Can you find the antique typewriter?

Baker Heritage Museum
2480 Grove St.
Baker City, OR 97814
541-523-9308

- Open March through October - 9:00 a.m. 4:00 p.m., Monday - Sunday
- Admission: Adults $7.00., Seniors (60+) $6.00, Children 12 and under are free.

☐ **Next Stop:** The Armstrong Nugget

One of the largest gold nuggets ever found in Oregon, weighing in at a whopping five pounds, is on display along with numerous smaller nuggets in the US Bank building across from the Geiser Grand Hotel. Open to viewing by the public during regular banking hours.

US Bank
2000 Main St.
Baker City, OR 97814
541-523-7791

☐ **Next Stop:** National Historic Oregon Trail Interpretive Center

The struggles, losses and joys of the pioneers who braved the Oregon Trail come to life at the National Historic Oregon Trail Interpretive Center. Located six miles NE of Baker City, at Exit 302 off I-84, the interpretive center presents impressive displays, multimedia exhibits, dioramas, interpretive programs and more, all of which immerse visitors in this important period of our state's history.

Oregon Trail Interpretive Center
22267 OR-86, Baker City, OR 97814
541-523-1843

- Located 6 Miles east of Baker City on Hwy 86
- Take Exit 302 when traveling I-84
- 9:00 a.m. – 6:00 p.m. Beginning mid-April - $8
- Closed Thanksgiving, Christmas Day, New Year's Day and during periods of severe weather.

☐ **Next Stop:** Horse Drawn Carriage Rides

Enjoy a 40 minute ride on an antique horse drawn vis-à-vis carriage through the historic sections of Baker City.

Arrangements may be made through the front desk of the Geiser Grand Hotel, (541-523-1889) as well as other hotels in town. In addition, you may call Ron or Lois Colton at 541-523-5701. They are happy to accommodate your start time, as well customize the length and destination of your trip. Base rates at press time are $35 per couple for a ½ hour ride.

☐ **Next Stop**: Return to Baker City, OR

Stay your second night at the Geiser Grand Hotel or The Wisdom House.

Notes

DAY FIVE

ELKHORN SCENIC BYWAY LOOP – TO UNION

Sumpter Valley Railroad 1890 - 1947

DAY 5
ELKHORN SCENIC BYWAY
LOOP - TO UNION, OR

Day 5 – Date: /   /

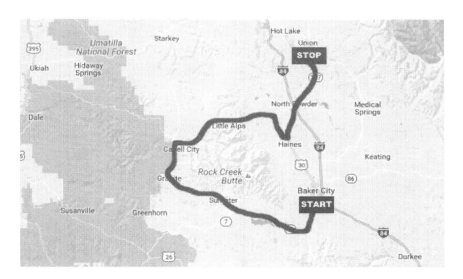

Summary: Where You're Going Today

- McEwen
- Sumpter (By steam train)
- Granite
- Anthony Lakes
- Haines
- Union

Today you will leave Baker City and journey clockwise on much of the Elkhorn Scenic Byway, a 118 mile paved route upon which you'll spy wildlife, board a massive gold-hunting dredge, ride aboard a classic old steam train and visit Haines, "The Biggest Little Town in Oregon." You'll finish by driving to Union, OR, where you'll stay in the Historic Union Hotel.

87

Today's Mileage: 118 Miles

Reservations Needed for This Segment:

- Sumpter Valley Railroad: Call 541-894-2268 to make reservations for a departure time. This is optional, as you may also buy tickets at the depot. Note that it can be difficult to get somebody to answer this phone.

- Peavy Cabin: While you will not be staying at the Peavy Cabin, you will be stopping by to get a look. Call the US Forest Service at 541-523-6391 to see if it is currently being rented. If it is not, then you can walk its grounds once you arrive.

  Note: The road to Peavy Cabin travels along the North Fork John Day River for its length. Take the time to park at the meadow, shortly after leaving NFD-73, and walk over to the river.

- Lodging: Historic Union Hotel: 541-562-1200

Note: *Much of today's trip hinges on the departure time you select for the Sumpter Valley Railroad excursion*, which departs from McEwen, OR and heads north to Sumpter, Oregon before returning to McEwen. See the information which follows.

Important: You will want to skip the "northern" part of today's route through the Anthony Lakes area if you are traveling between October and May and there is *any* snow still remaining on the road.

This route is closed between Granite, OR and north to Anthony Lakes during the winter, opening approximately mid- to late-May, depending upon the year's snow melt, and closing again in early- to mid-October/November, depending upon winter conditions.

For the latest road conditions, call:

- The Wallowa Whitman Ranger Station – 541-523-6391
- Oregon Department of Transportation - 800-977-6368

Important: If you are traveling this road during the shoulder months, it is important to carry chains and a shovel of some kind in case you become stuck in the snow. Snow, especially in the spring, can grab the underside of your car like cement, requiring you to dig out the *entire* underside in order to break free, which takes approximately two hours. (Don't ask me how I know this.) There is no cell service in portions of this route. It is tempting to try to make your way through short sections of road covered in snow, but this can be a serious mistake, as we've seen even moderately deep patches of snow (6" – 8") across the road thwart even the sturdiest of 4 x 4s. Be responsible and come prepared with travel tools, as well as food and warm clothing, if you are traveling this route in May or June, or late September or October. In the event you do encounter snow blocking your route, simply return via the route you came and enjoy a leisurely dinner in Baker City, instead of spending your time digging out your car...as a rain cloud rolls in.

 **Before You Leave:**

Fill your gas tank in Baker City, OR

Start

As you make your way along the Elkhorn Scenic Byway south out of Baker City, you'll first travel along the route you took into town the night before, that being Hwy 7. Follow this west as it makes its way from grasslands to a ponderosa forest, all while traveling along the Powder River, which is an excellent fishery holding hatchery and native trout.

First Stop: McEwen, OR – Sumpter Valley Railroad

This stop is guaranteed to be a highlight of your trip, giving you a taste of actual Oregon history as you board an authentic 1890 narrow gauge steam train and travel back in time. You'll hear the chuff-chuff-chuff of the powerful locomotive and the shrill of its steam whistle as you ply the rails from McEwen, OR to the historic mining town of Sumpter, OR and back. Better yet, you can even ride in the cab!

The train makes round-trip journeys from McEwen, OR north to Sumpter, OR during select weekends and major holidays from Memorial Day Weekend through the last weekend in September. During some weekends, the train will make two round trips, creating four departure times; two from McEwen and two from Sumpter, and during other weekends, which correspond with a large flea market in Sumpter, the train will make three round trips, thereby creating six different departure times, three from each town.

Visit their web site at www.SumpterValleyRailroad.org to learn more about the train and its schedule during your visit.

Our recommendation is to enjoy this unique Oregon experience as follows:

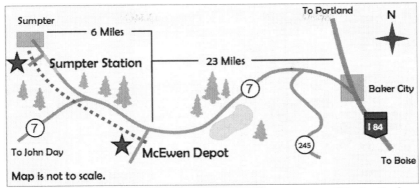

Map courtesy of Taylor Rush

1. Depart Baker City and drive 23 miles southwest along the Elkhorn Scenic Byway (Hwy 7) to arrive at the Sumpter Valley Railroad depot in McEwen by 9:30 a.m. for the 10:00 a.m. train to Sumpter. This will give you enough time to purchase your tickets and explore the train up close. Tickets as of press time are $21.00 round-trip for adults, ages 5 – 15 are $12.00, and children ages 4 and under travel at no charge. The travel time aboard the train from McEwen to Sumpter is approximately 45 minutes.

2. Ride the train north to Sumpter, depart and explore the Sumpter Valley Dredge State Heritage Area, showcasing the fascinating Sumpter Valley Gold Dredge.

3. Board the 11:30 a.m. or 12:00 noon train back to McEwen, depending upon the schedule for that weekend.

Note that after you arrive back at McEwen via the train ride, you will then be driving north to Sumpter, where you will have additional time to explore the town, its shops and flea market, which runs every Memorial Day, 4th of July and Labor Day weekend.

You may either call the Sumpter Valley Railroad at 541-894-2268 or email Reservations@SumpterValleyRailroad.org to make reservations. Note: We tried many times to make our reservations prior to Memorial Day Weekend using these two contacts but never received a response, so we bought our tickets, including the General Cab Pass, at the train depot in McEwen, which worked out fine.

Ride in the Cab of a Steam Locomotive!

Note: *Also available on a limited first-come, first-served basis is a ride up front in the locomotive with the engineers, a truly unique Oregon experience.* Cab passes may be purchased for $45 for adults or $30 for passengers ages 5 to 17, and this provides a one-way trip in the locomotive cab, a return trip on board the passenger train and a one-year membership in the Sumpter Valley Railroad. Closed toe shoes are required, and be mindful of where the Tender car joins the locomotive cab while riding, or you could crush a toe. (Don't let that stop you from riding in the cab!)

Driving Directions:

Depart Baker City and drive The Elkhorn Scenic Byway (Hwy 7) southwest 23 miles to McEwen. Turn left off the highway at the sign for the Sumpter Valley Railroad and park in their large parking lot near the restored train depot.

Sumpter Valley Railroad Depot
12259 Huckleberry Loop
Baker City, OR 97814

Note: Though it is called the Sumpter Valley Railroad, the depot in the town of McEwen is the originating depot for the railway and all trains from here are round-trip to Sumpter and back unless otherwise noted.

☐ **Next Stop**: Sumpter Valley Gold Dredge State Heritage Site – Via the Sumpter Valley Railroad

Upon your arrival in Sumpter via the Sumpter Valley Railroad, you'll find nearby the Sumpter Valley Gold Dredge State Heritage Site, showcasing the massive Sumpter Valley Gold Dredge. One of three dredges of its kind, it extracted gold throughout the area from 1935 until 1954, when its rapacious boom carrying 72 one-ton buckets fell silent. It then sat in a state of growing disrepair until 1995, when the dredge and over 93 acres were purchased for preservation and restoration. There is no fee to visit this site.

Sumpter Valley Gold Dredge
211 Austin St.
Sumpter, OR 97877
541-894-2486

☐ **Next Stop**: Sumpter Flea Market

During Memorial Day, 4th of July and Labor Day weekends, Sumpter comes alive with a large flea market, which hums with the activity of 150 vendors offering antiques, collectibles and foods of all kinds. You may find little of value, or perhaps a treasure or two, as we did.

For information, contact the City of Sumpter: 541-894-2314

☐ Next Stop: Hand Dipped Corn Dogs

It's been a while since you've had a hand dipped corn dog, hasn't it? Now is the time to fix that. Stop by the Hand Dipped Corn Dog cart on the main route through town and ask Mary to fix you a delicious all beef corn dog to enjoy while you people-watch in Sumpter. Bottles of ice cold water are also available.

☐ Next Stop: Granite, OR

With a population of approximately 40 people, the small town of Granite, Oregon has a gold mining history reaching back to 1862, when gold was discovered in Granite Creek. There are no stops in Granite, but it is interesting to drive through to see some of the old buildings.

Driving Directions: Continue driving northwest on the Elkhorn Scenic Byway until reaching Granite, OR.

www.Discover-Oregon.com

☐ **Next Stop**: Peavy Cabin

Turn off the Elkhorn Scenic Byway and follow a dusty road meandering through alpine meadows and forests to find Peavy Cabin. Built in 1934, this classic single-room log cabin is set in a beautiful high alpine valley along the North Fork John Day River.

Call the US Forest Service at 541-523-6391 prior to driving the Elkhorn Scenic Byway to ask if the cabin is currently being rented. If its not, then once you arrive, walk past the gate and get a look inside. If it is being rented, you can still get a good look at it from its closed gate.

Note: This sparsely furnished cabin is available for rent during the months of July through October. Learn more by calling 541-523-6391.

Driving Directions: Driving north on the Elkhorn Scenic Byway, turn right at the North Fork John Day Campground / junction for Anthony Lakes, where you'll continue on The Elkhorn Scenic Byway / NFD 73. At 4.7 miles from the turn, you'll see a small sign for Peavy Cabin. Turn right onto the gravel road at the sign, NF-360, and follow this 2.8 miles to the cabin. Note: Some online directions will list the gravel road as NF-380.

Next Stop: Anthony Lakes Ski Area

Anthony Lakes Hike

An easy one mile loop trail around 7,140' Anthony Lake provides hikers with beautiful alpine views of nearby 8,342' Gunsight Mountain in the northern Elkhorn Range. The view seen here is from near the parking area.

- Takes approximately ½ Hour
- Open Late-May/June through October.

Note: Mountain bikers will enjoy a growing number of routes for all skill levels out of the Anthony Lake Ski Area, including the Anthony Lake Loop for beginners.

Driving Directions: Continue north on the Elkhorn Scenic Byway / NFD 73. Opposite the North Fork John Day Campground, the byway turns right / east. (Note: Continuing straight without turning will take you onto the Blue Mountain Scenic Byway / NF 52, which is the route you drove the other day from Ukiah.) Follow the Elkhorn Scenic Byway 16 miles to the Anthony Lakes Ski Area and the Anthony Lake Campground. Turn right at the campground sign and, after about 100 yards, stay to the right and continue to the picnic area. Parking is available on the left at the large wooden picnic gazebo. Day use fees are $5.00 per vehicle. Note: There is no access to Anthony Lakes from the western portion of the Elkhorn Scenic Byway from approximately mid-October until mid-May, when the road is closed due to snow. For current road conditions, contact the Wallowa Whitman Ranger Station – 541-523-6391.

☐ Next Stop: Haines, OR – "The Biggest Little Town in Oregon"

☐ Haines Stop: Eastern Oregon Museum

Features an extensive collection of pioneer antiques, photos and documents showcasing the history of Haines, Baker County and Eastern Oregon.

Eastern Oregon Museum
610 3rd Street
Haines, OR 97833
541-856-3233

- Open mid-May through mid-September
- Thursday – Saturday – 10:00 a.m. – 4:00 p.m.
- Sunday 12:30 noon – 3:30 p.m.
- If you are arriving outside of these hours, you may call and schedule an appointment to see the museum.

☐ Haines Stop: Haines Steakhouse

A western themed restaurant offering high quality steaks, seafood, salads, and gourmet desserts.

Haines Steakhouse
910 Front Street
Haines, OR 97833
541-856-3639

- Reservations are not required
- Open Monday, Wednesday, Thursday & Friday: 4:30 p.m.
- Open Saturday: 3:30 p.m.

- Open Sunday: 12:30 p.m.
- Closed Tuesdays
- Closes sometime between 8:00 p.m. and 9:00 p.m., depending upon how busy it is that day.

Driving Directions: Continue east on the Elkhorn Scenic Byway from the Anthony Lakes Ski Area to Haines, OR. (39 Miles)

TONIGHT'S LODGING
HISTORIC UNION HOTEL -
UNION, OR

You'll encounter two different kinds of hotels during your Discover Oregon journey. The first is the hotel built at the turn of the previous century, which has been updated with modern amenities, and the second is the same kind of hotel, but maintained with its historic period-specific look and ambiance. The Historic Union Hotel fits the latter.

First opened in 1921, its lobby welcomes guests into another era reaching back nearly 100 years. Massive dark wooden columns flank a long reception desk showcasing antiques from the hotel's past, while nearby a large buffalo head hangs on a wall above another old typewriter. Upstairs, 15 themed rooms invite guests to leave behind their phones and devices to relax with family, friends and a good book.

Note: Be sure to see the historical items under glass at the reception desk, as well as the small reading library on the second floor.

Historic Union Hotel
326 N. Main Street
Union, OR 97883
541-562-1200
HistoricUnionHotel@gmail.com

- Open year round. Located on the main road through Union.

Driving Directions: Leave the Elkhorn Scenic Byway at Haines, OR and drive north out of town on Front Street / Hwy 30 to I-84. Crossing under I-84, you'll be on 2nd Street. Follow 2nd Street as it turns into the Hwy 237 / La Grande-Baker Highway. Follow this as it turns into the Grande Tour Scenic Byway, eventually reaching Union, OR as South Main Street. The Union Historic Hotel is on your left as you make your way north through town.

Notes

DAY SIX

UNION TO JOSEPH

Chief Joseph - Leader of the Nez Perce. 1840 – 1904

DAY 6
UNION TO JOSEPH

Day 6 – Date: /   /

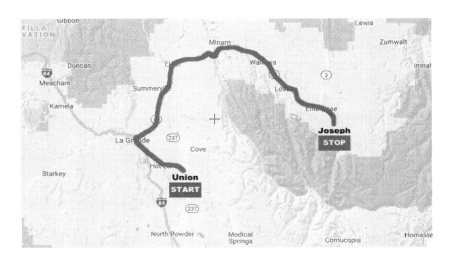

Summary: Where You're Going Today

- Union
- La Grande
- Wallowa
- Enterprise
- Joseph

Tonight's Lodging:

- The 1910 Historic Enterprise House B&B *or*
- The Bronze Antler Inn B&B *or*
- The Wallowa Lake Lodge

Reservations Needed for This Segment:

Choose a single lodging spot for the next 3 nights or mix it up between each location:

- 1910 Historic Enterprise House B & B: 541-426-4238
  or
- The Bronze Antler Inn: 541-432-0230
  or
- The Wallowa Lake Lodge & Cabins: 541-432-9821

- Sunrise Iron Antique Tractor Collection:
  - 541-426-4407
  - 541-263-0755
  - Reservations are preferred, but are not mandatory

Today, you'll connect two Oregon scenic byways to create one single journey. Traveling northwest out of Union, you'll head towards La Grande on a portion of the **Grande Tour Route Scenic Byway** before turning northeast towards Imbler, OR, where you'll then connect with the **Hells Canyon Scenic Byway** as it takes you to Joseph, OR. Along the way, you'll traverse hay fields, pine forests and open prairies before arriving at the base of the beautiful "Oregon Alps".

Today's Mileage: 89 Miles

For the latest road conditions, openings and closures, contact:

- La Grande Ranger District: 541-963-7186
- Wallowa-Whitman Forest Headquarters: 541-523-6391

 **Note:** Fill your gas tank across from the hotel before leaving Union. Gas is also available along today's route.

www.Discover-Oregon.com

Grande Tour Route Scenic Byway

☐ **First Stop**: Breakfast at the Historic Union Hotel

Begin your day by having breakfast in the dining room of the Historic Union Hotel. As an option, you may wait to have breakfast at the Hot Lake Springs Resort & Hotel, which is five miles into today's journey.

☐ **Union Stop**: Union County Museum

After breakfast, drive south on Main Street to visit the Union County Museum and its collection of photos and artifacts from Union County's past.

Union County Museum
331 S. Main Street
Union, OR 97883
541-562-6003
ucmuseumoregon.com

- Open Mother's Day through October 1st
- Monday – Saturday, 10:00 a.m. – 4:00 p.m.
- Admission: $5 for Adults, $4 for Seniors, $3 for Students – Children under six are free.

☐ **Next Stop**: Hot Lake Springs Resort & Hotel

The historic Hot Lake Springs Resort & Hotel makes up the town of Hot Lake Springs, OR in its entirety. Once a popular stop on the Oregon Trail, this historic Colonial Revival building dating back to 1906 suffered a major fire in 1934, during the great depression, which destroyed half of the building, as well as ceased all operations. Over time, ensuing owners attempted to revive the business in various forms, but all efforts failed and the building fell into a state of neglect and disrepair. Abandoned, vandalized and looted, the resort was purchased by the Manuel family and an extensive restoration effort was begun in 2003, leading to its reopening seven years later. Today, the resort and its complex offers visitors a glimpse into the past as it hosts overnight stays, fine dining, group and event activities, and more.

Hot Lake Springs Resort & Hotel
66172 OR-203
La Grande, OR 97850
541-963-4685

Driving Directions:

Drive northwest out of Union on OR 203 / La Grande-Baker Hwy towards La Grande, and stop at the town of Hot Lake Springs, (5 miles) which consists solely of the Hot Lake Springs Resort & Hotel.

Note: As you leave Union and veer left onto Hwy 203, you'll see signs for OR 237 heading right / east, which heads east and then north out of Union. This will also take you to the Hells Canyon Scenic Byway / Hwy 82 via gravel roads, connecting at Island City, OR, but it will bypass the Hot Lake Springs Resort Hotel stop.

Return to Route:

Leaving Hot Lake, OR, continue driving 9 miles northwest on Hwy OR 203 to La Grande, where you'll then travel northeast on Hwy 82 to the town of Imbler, OR. Connect with the Hells Canyon Scenic Byway / Hwy 82 at the town of Imbler and follow this to Joseph, OR, your destination for the day.

Hells Canyon Scenic Byway

Travel Northeast on the Hells Canyon Scenic Byway / Hwy 82 out of Imbler, OR.

☐ **Next Stop**: Eagle Cap Excursion Train

Eagle Cap Wilderness Train
300 Depot Street
Elgin, OR 97827
800-323-7330

Plying the tracks between Elgin, OR and Minam, OR, the powerful diesel engine of the Eagle Cap Excursion Train takes visitors into the Eastern Oregon wilderness along the scenic Grande Ronde River before turning upstream along the Wallowa River to Minam. Trips tailored for Mother's Day, wine & cheese aficionados and history buffs await visitors roughly every other week between early May through late October.

Departs from the Elgin Depot. 40 Miles round-trip. Departure time: 10:00 a.m., but this time varies. Allow 4 – 5 hours round-trip, depending upon the route taken. Adults: $70, Seniors: $65, Youth 3 – 16: $35 – Kids under 3 ride for free. A box lunch is included. Reservations are recommended. To make reservations, call Alegre Travel at 800-323-7330 or send an email to Train@AlegreTravel.com. To learn more and to see the train schedule, visit www.EagleCapTrainRides.com.

☐ **Next Stop**: Minam, OR

As you enter the town of Elgin, you'll see a small sign pointing north, which reads "Minam State Park, 2 Miles". As a short but interesting side trip, turn left off OR-82 and drive along the beautiful Wallowa River to the State Park. Park here and walk down by the river.

☐ **Next Stop**: Enterprise, OR - Sunrise Iron Antique Tractor Collection

Located on Sunrise Road, just west of Enterprise, OR, is Sunrise Iron, an amazing collection of 35 beautifully restored antique tractors dating as far back as 1835...over 180 years ago. Owned and curated by Erl McLaughlin, the collection is housed in a large 40' x 220' metal shop on Mr. McLaughlin's farm. It's an informal operation, so to see this tribute to agricultural heritage, simply give Erl a call and arrange a time to stop by. He greatly enjoys showing visitors his collection.

Sunrise Iron
65708 Sunrise Road
Enterprise, OR 97828
541-426-4407
541-263-0755
Info@SunriseIron.com

Driving Directions:

As you drive south on Hwy 82 and approach Enterprise, turn right / south onto Sunrise Road. Admission is free, but donations of $5 or more for future projects are gladly accepted. Please be courteous and call in advance, if possible.

☐ **Next Stop**: Forest Service Visitor Center – Joseph, OR

Stop in to see an interesting collection of Indian artifacts, natural history displays and a scenic view of the Wallowa Mountains from the observation deck. Also available are maps, recreation passes, information brochures and more.

Forest Service Visitor Center
201 E. Second Street
Joseph, OR 97846
541-426-5546

- Open 8:00 a.m. – 5:00 p.m., Monday - Saturday

TONIGHT'S LODGING - THREE CHOICES NEAR JOSEPH, OR

For tonight's lodging, you have three excellent choices in the area from which to choose...

1. The 1910 Enterprise House Historic Bed & Breakfast
2. The Bronze Antler Inn Bed & Breakfast
3. The Wallowa Lake Lodge & Cabins

You will be making reservations for 3 nights. Note: You may wish to consider staying at more than one location.

☐ 1) The 1910 Historic Enterprise House B&B

A Colonial Revival home recognized as one of the 25 Great Oregon Hotels & Resorts, the 1910 Historic Enterprise House Bed & Breakfast offers guests "a unique blend of country peacefulness and Southern hospitality."

Look for a sign on your right, as you begin to make your way east out of Enterprise towards Joseph, which instructs you to turn at the next left to find the Enterprise House Bed & Breakfast.

1910 Historic Enterprise House Bed & Breakfast
508 First South Street
Enterprise, OR 97828
541-426-4238
www.EnterpriseHouseBnB.com

☐ 2) The Bronze Antler Bed & Breakfast

Located in Joseph, OR, at the base of the Wallowa Mountains, is the finely appointed Bronze Antler Bed & Breakfast. A Craftsman style home with resplendent grounds, it welcomes you with its cozy charm, perfect after  a day of exploring. Being a Bed & Breakfast, you'll begin each day with a meal fit for a world traveler, yet made with local ingredients. And if you're lucky, you'll be joined by other guests, giving you an opportunity to meet fellow travelers and share your stories of Oregon adventures.

Only a short walk away is the "downtown" area of Joseph. Home to a thriving art community, it hosts numerous art galleries, dramatic bronze sculptures on every corner and dining to suit everyone's needs.

Note: The Bronze Antler Inn caters primarily to adults, with a minimum of two night stays over the weekends. Single weekend nights may be available from time to time.

> Bronze Antler Bed & Breakfast
> 309 S. Main Street
> Joseph, OR 97846
> 541-432-0230

- www.BronzeAntler.com
- Info@BronzeAntler.com

Note: The Bronze Antler B & B offers a Tesla charging station, and the town of Joseph offers a laundromat.

☐ 3) The Wallowa Lake Lodge & Cabins

Stay on the shores of Wallowa Lake in the historic Wallowa Lake Lodge and Cabins. Built in 1923, the era of Model T auto-touring, the lodge has a rustic National Park Lodge feel to it, complete with a large stone fireplace, and offers 22 rooms with private baths. In addition, visitors may choose from any of the eight separate cabins near the Wallowa Lake shore. The Camas Dining Room offers outstanding Northwest cuisine for breakfast and dinner.

Lodge rooms are available May 15 through the end of October, while the eight cabins are available year-round. The lodge, cabins and grounds are all no-smoking areas, and pets are not allowed. Learn more at www.WallowaLakeLodge.com

Photo Copyright David Jensen

Wallowa Lake Lodge
60060 Wallowa Lake Hwy
Joseph, OR 97846

541-432-9821
WallowaLakeLodge.com

www.Discover-Oregon.com

Notes

EXPLORE JOSEPH, OR & WALLOWA LAKE

"The first white men of your people who came to our country were named Lewis and Clark. They brought many things which our people had never seen. They talked straight and our people gave them a great feast as proof that their hearts were friendly."

Chief Joseph

DAY 7
EXPLORE JOSEPH, OR
& WALLOWA LAKE

Day 7 – Date: /   /

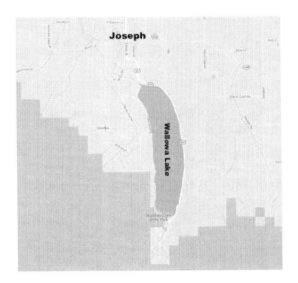

Today you spend the day exploring the Joseph, OR area and then stay your second night at your current lodging.

Reservations Needed for this Segment:

- Valley Bronze Foundry Tour: 541-432-7445
- Joseph Branch Rail Riders: 541-786-6149

☐ **Joseph Activity**: Explore Joseph

Begin the day by walking through Joseph for a couple of hours while exploring its collection of art galleries, shops, museums and restaurants.

☐ Joseph Activity: Wallowa County Museum

A fascinating collection of historical artifacts, photos and documents reveals the history of Wallowa County.

110 S. Main Street
Joseph, OR 97846
541-432-6095

An invitation to a public hanging

- Open 10:00 a.m. – 4:00 p.m. from Memorial Day weekend through the third weekend in September. Adults $4, Seniors $3.00, Students aged 7 – 17 $2.00, Children six and under are free.

☐ Joseph Activity: Bronze and Art Galleries

Joseph is home to a half dozen or more bronze and art galleries featuring many different local, regional and national artists, as well as a handful of unique shops. Walk through Joseph and stop in at those which catch your eye. Gallery owners are more  than happy to provide information on pieces of art or the artists themselves. Most galleries open at 10:00 a.m.

☐ Joseph Activity: Valley Bronze Foundry Tour

Valley Bronze of Oregon offers tours of its foundry once each day beginning at 11:00 a.m.. Lasting one to one and a half hours, you'll learn about the fascinating process of sculpting bronze into works of art. Tickets are available at the Valley Bronze Gallery on Main Street in Joseph and may be presented at the nearby foundry before your tour begins. $15 for Adults, $10 for Seniors or Military, and children under 10 are free.

Valley Bronze Gallery
18 South Main Street
Joseph, OR 97846
541-432-7445

Valley Bronze Foundry
307 West Alder Street
Joseph, OR 97846
541-432-7551

☐ Joseph Activity: Arrowhead Chocolates

What better way to enjoy the "Oregon Alps" than with chocolate?

Stop in at the family owned Arrowhead Chocolates on Main Street to indulge in award-winning truffles, caramels, nut clusters, chocolate bark and other decadent confections, all made by hand in the small shop. Then, with your selection in hand, grab a table and enjoy your choice of Stumptown Coffees, smooth hot chocolate, apple cider and perhaps a savory biscuit or freshly baked cookie. It's truly a memorable taste of Oregon.

Arrowhead Chocolates
100 N Main Street
Joseph, OR 97846
541-432-2871

- Open Monday thru Sunday – 7:00 a.m. to 5:00 p.m.

117

 **Joseph** **Activity**: Joseph Branch Railriders

A fun Oregon adventure! Sit down aboard a two-seater Railrider and pedal from Joseph to Enterprise along the old Joseph Branch rail line. Traveling at a casual pace down a slight 1.5% grade, you'll "ride the rails" while  enjoying views of the summits of the Eagle Cap Wilderness. Along the way, you'll make friends with like-minded adventurers before using "a little more energy as you pedal back to Joseph."

Each Railrider carries two people, but singles are welcome. A guide will accompany each group. Helmets are optional and available for use. $24 for ages 12 and older, $12 for those under 12. Young children are asked to use a car seat if they cannot reach the pedals.

- Departs at 9:00 a.m., noon and 3:00 p.m.
- Begins late-May and continues through the first weekend in October. Call for exact days and departure times. Reservations are encouraged and may be made online at www.JBRailriders.com

You'll find the ticket and departure location located here:

501 West Alder St.
Joseph, OR 97846
541-786-6149
JBRailriders.com
JBRailriders@gmail.com

☐ Joseph Activity: Hurricane Creek Hike

Hike into the base of the Wallowa Mountains on this scenic 6.5 mile round-trip trail along Hurricane Creek. Stunning views of 9,844' Sacajawea Peak accompany you as you make your way through alpine meadows at the base of granite cliffs. Reach Slippery Rock Canyon and enjoy the waterfalls, as well as the now turbulent Hurricane Creek as it twists and dives through a narrow gorge.

Fee: $5.00 per vehicle per day – Available at the trailhead. The trail opens in late May or June, depending upon the snow melt.

Driving Directions: From Main Street in Joseph, travel west on Airport Lane for approximately 1.5 miles until the road transitions into Hurricane Creek Road. Continue for another 0.5 miles to the intersection by the Hurricane Creek Grange. Turn left here onto County Road 521, also known as Hurricane Creek Road, and follow this 3.7 miles until it terminates at the Hurricane Creek Trailhead.

☐ Joseph Activity: Explore Wallowa Lake and the Wallowa Lake Tramway

- Wallowa Lake – Drive the eastern edge of Wallowa Lake and explore the south end of the lake, Wallowa Lake State Park, and the Wallowa Lake Marina, where visitors can rent row boats, kayaks, SUP boards and more.

- Wallowa Lake Family Activities – The south end of Wallowa Lake is home to numerous family related businesses, including miniature golf, horseback rides, bumper boats, go carts, paddle boats and more.

☐ **Wallowa Lake Activity**: Kayak and Boat Rentals

Kayak and boat rentals are available at the Wallowa Lake Marina. See rental rates online at WallowaLakeMarina.com

Wallowa Lake Marina
South end of Wallowa Lake
72214 Marina Lane
Joseph, OR 97846
541-432-9115

- Seasonal Hours:
- Early May: 10:00 a.m. – 6:00 p.m.
- Memorial Day – Labor Day: 8:00 a.m. – 8:00 p.m.
- After Labor Day – Sept. 15: 10:00 a.m. – 6:00 p.m.
- Open 7 days a week
- Closed for the season beginning September 15th

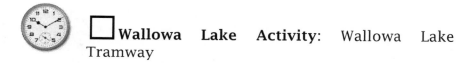 ☐ **Wallowa Lake Activity**: Wallowa Lake Tramway

 Take a 15 minute gondola ride aboard the steepest tram in North America to the lofty height of 8,150' to experience a stunning close up view of the Wallowa Mountains and the Eagle Cap Wilderness. Hike to the summit of Mt. Howard or any of the nearby summit area overlooks, enjoy an alpine picnic or simply dine at the Summit Grill. Operates only during weekends in late May, and then daily from June to October 1st.

Ticket prices are $35 for Adults, $32 for Seniors 65 and older, $29 for Students ages 12 – 17 with ID, $23 for Youth ages 4 – 11 and $6 for children 3 and under.

Wallowa Lake Tramway
59919 Wallowa Lake Highway
Joseph, OR 97846
541-432-5331

Note: The summit area is at an elevation of 8,150', so it is advisable to bring warm clothing, a warm coat, sunglasses and sunscreen.

Interpretive snowshoe trips are offered in May, (snow permitting) and daily tandem Paragliding trips are offered from July until early September. Call for information and conditions: 541-432-5331.

Driving Directions: While the Wallowa Lake Tramway's address is "in" Joseph, it is actually located at the south end of Wallowa Lake, 6 miles south of Joseph. Travel south out of Joseph along OR-351 until it turns into Powerhouse Road. Follow this approximately ½ mile past the south end of Wallowa Lake until you spot the Wallowa Lake Tramway on your left.

☐ **Wallowa Lake Activity**: Summit Grill

Dine at the Summit Grill, the Northwest's highest restaurant at 8,150'. Featuring Northwest cuisine, the Summit Grill offers lunch, snacks and both hot and cold drinks, beer and wine, all in an alpine setting with stunning views of Wallowa Lake, as well as the nearby granite peaks of the Wallowa Mountains. And for those who wish to hike in the area, box lunches are available.

Directions: The Summit Grill can be found at the top of the Wallowa Lake Tramway.

- 541-432-5331
- Open 10:00 a.m. – 4:00 p.m.
- Breakfast is served 10:00 a.m. – 12:00 p.m. – Beginning early June

- Open Memorial Day through Labor Day, approximately mid-May to early October
- Reservations are not required
- Open in all weather conditions, unless winds are from the north or south at 33 mph or above

☐ **Wallowa Lake Activity**: Chief Joseph Trail

The Chief Joseph Trail makes for a perfect late afternoon or early evening activity. Making its way through the forest at the south end of Wallowa Lake, it crosses the West Fork of the Wallowa River before taking you to BC Falls and dramatic views of the area. 3+ miles roundtrip.

Driving & Hiking Directions: Drive Power House Road at the south end of Wallowa Lake to where it terminates at the Wallowa Lake Trailhead. Hike the West Fork Wallowa River Trail #1820 for ¼ mile until it meets with the Chief Joseph Trail. Here, follow the fork right and cross a bridge above the West Fork of the Wallowa River at the half-mile mark. Continue another 1+ miles to BC Falls, which cascades across the trail. If the water is running high, this makes for an excellent destination and turnaround point. However, if the water is running low and you feel you can *safely* navigate the cascade, then cross and continue for another 200 yards, where you'll find a large rock outcrop with a beautiful view of Wallowa Lake to the north.

 **Wallowa Lake Activity**: Dine at Wallowa Lake Lodge

The Camas Dining Room offers outstanding Northwest cuisine for breakfast and dinner. Enjoy your meal and then stroll the park-like lakeside grounds, or simply drop into an oversized chair and enjoy a cup of coffee and a good book in front of the large stone fireplace.

Wallowa Lake Lodge & Cabins
60060 Wallowa Lake Hwy
Joseph, OR 97846
541-432-9821

- Breakfast: 7:30 a.m. – 11:00 a.m.
- Dinner: 5:30 p.m. – 9:00 p.m.

Driving Directions: Drive south out of Joseph on Main Street, which turns into Hwy 351 / Wallowa Lake Hwy. Follow this as it makes its way to the lodge at the south end of Wallowa Lake.

www.Discover-Oregon.com

Notes

DAY EIGHT

EXPLORE THE ZUMWALT PRAIRIE PRESERVE

"We have been traveling among the hills and the monotony has been relieved by the ever varying beauty of the scenery and the pleasantness of the weather."

Elizabeth Wood – July 4, 1851

DAY 8
EXPLORE THE
ZUMWALT PRAIRIE PRESERVE

Day 8 – Date: /   /

Today you drive north to explore the Zumwalt Prairie Preserve and then stay your third night at your current lodging.

Subtle in its silent beauty and expansive grandeur, the remote Zumwalt Prairie Preserve is the largest remaining expanse of prairie left in North America. At 51 square miles in size, you'll marvel at the "silence of distance" as you gaze over the grasslands which stretch to distant horizons, all beneath an endless sky which competes for your attention.

Be sure to fill your gas tank in Joseph before leaving for today's adventure.

Important: You will be traveling into a very remote area today with no cell coverage or services available. The roads will primarily be gravel, and they are fine for passenger cars with good tires. It is wise to bring food and water in case you run into trouble of some kind. If, for some reason you do need assistance, expect cars to pass by periodically during the spring, summer and fall months.

Generally speaking, though they are not plowed or maintained, most roads in the Zumwalt Prairie Preserve are accessible from spring through fall, with access to the prairie also available throughout the winter, provided a recent snowfall has not occurred. Note that even with lesser snow amounts, snow drifts can be an issue. Access to the Buckhorn Fire Lookout is generally not available during the winter months.

For the latest road conditions, openings and closures, contact:

- Eagle Cap Ranger District: 541-426-4978
- Wallowa-Whitman National Forest office: 541-523-6391

☐ **Zumwalt Prairie Activity**: Drive to Buckhorn Fire Lookout

This exploration to a remote yet uniquely sublime part of Oregon makes for a full and adventurous day. Leave Joseph and drive north on Hwy 82 / The Hells Canyon Scenic Byway, where you'll journey through the open grasslands and forests of the Zumwalt Prairie Preserve for nearly 40 miles before reaching the Buckhorn Fire Lookout with its amazing Grand Canyon-esque view over the Lower Imnaha River Canyon thousands of feet below. Plan on bringing a picnic lunch and a blanket to sit upon to enjoy the endless views and quiet beauty.

Distance: Joseph, OR to Buckhorn Lookout: 42 Miles - Opens in late May / June. No fee required. Plan on 3.5 to 4.0 hours from Joseph to the Buckhorn Fire Lookout.

Driving Directions: Reset your odometer at the corner of Wallowa Ave. and Main Street in Joseph, OR.

Drive north from Joseph on Hwy 82 towards Enterprise. When you reach Eggleson Corner at 2.9 miles, (Located 3.5 miles south of Enterprise) turn right / east onto Eggleson Lane, which directs you onto Cow Creek Road and into the heart of the Zumwalt Prairie Preserve. Follow Cow Creek Road east and then, as the road begins to turn north, head right onto Zumwalt Road at the 8 mile mark. Follow this NE, as it turns into the Zumwalt-Buckhorn Road, until you reach the turn off to Buckhorn Lookout at approximately 40.5 miles. Turn right onto NF-780 and follow this a little over one mile to the lookout. Note: You will transition from open grasslands to forest as you make your way there. Be sure to bring your binoculars and your camera.

☐ Zumwalt Prairie Activity: Stop, Look and Listen

One of the marvels of the Zumwalt Prairie Preserve is its silence. Being so remote, there is little in the way of noise-generating activities nearby. Make it a point to stop your car, get out and appreciate the silence, which is punctuated only by the occasional melodious call of the Oregon State Bird, the Western Meadowlark.

In addition to songbirds, the preserve is home to an abundance of wildlife. As you make your way through the preserve, be ever watchful, as animals of all kinds can appear suddenly wherever you travel. Watch for deer, elk, coyotes, cougars, hawks, Golden Eagles and even black bears as they dig for roots in the grasslands. We saw a young bear right next to the road during our visit!

Note: If you are traveling in the spring, you'll find the prairies and forests filled with over 100 kinds of colorful wildflowers, all tended by nearly 100 native bee species and 57 native butterfly species.

☐ Zumwalt Prairie Activity: Hike Patti's Trail

There are a number of two to three mile hikes throughout the Zumwalt Prairie Preserve, and the scenic Patti's Trail is a perfect excursion conveniently located on the way to Buckhorn Fire Lookout. A 2.3 mile loop through the open native prairie takes you through knee high grass and wildflowers as it winds its way to the headwaters of Camp Creek.

Driving Directions: Reset your odometer at the corner of Wallowa Ave. and Main Street in Joseph, OR.

Drive north from Joseph on Hwy 82 / The Hells Canyon Scenic Byway towards Enterprise. When you reach Eggleson Corner at 2.9 miles, (Located 3.5 miles south of Enterprise) turn right / east onto Eggleson Lane, which directs you onto Cow Creek Road. Follow Cow Creek Road east and then, as the road begins to turn north, head right onto Zumwalt Road at the 8 mile mark. Follow this NE, as it turns into the Zumwalt-Buckhorn Road and continues into the Zumwalt Prairie Preserve. Once you reach Duckett Road at just beyond 22 miles, turn right and follow this 1.4 miles to the Duckett Barn parking area, which is marked with a large interpretive kiosk. You'll find the trailhead sign north of the road.

www.Discover-Oregon.com

Notes

DAY NINE

JOSEPH TO HELLS CANYON & HELLS CANYON TO PRAIRIE CITY

"There is some of the largest rattle snakes in this region I ever saw, being from 8 to 12 ft. long, and about as large as a man's leg about the knee. This is no fiction at all."

Amelia Hadley – July 19, 1851

DAY 9
JOSEPH TO HELLS CANYON
& PRAIRIE CITY

Day 9 – Date: / /

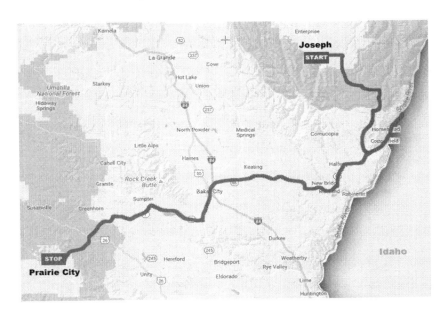

Summary: Where You're Going Today

- Hells Canyon
- Halfway
- Baker City
- Whitney
- Prairie City

Tonight's Lodging:

- Historic Hotel Prairie

Today's Mileage: 250 Miles

Today's journey takes you along three Oregon Scenic Byways, starting with the remainder of the Hells Canyon Scenic Byway. Traveling from Joseph, you'll drive along the byway to Hells Canyon, then on to Halfway, OR before finishing your day at the beautifully renovated Historic Hotel Prairie in Prairie City, OR.

Note: This portion of the Hells Canyon Scenic Byway is as seasonal road. As such, it opens sometime between early May to early June, once the snow melts and the road is cleared of any trees and debris that fell over the winter. It then closes to cars again sometime in October or November, when the snow begins to fall again. The road is not plowed or maintained over the winter. For the latest road conditions, openings and closures, contact:

- Eagle Cap Ranger District: 541-426-4978
- Wallowa-Whitman National Forest office: 541-523-6391

Reservations Needed for This Segment:

- Historic Hotel Prairie: 541-820-4800
- Hells Canyon Jet Boats: 541-785-3352

Before You Leave:

Fill your gas tank in Joseph, OR before leaving. You'll be driving in some remote areas, but there is also gas along the way.

☐ **Hells Canyon Activity**: Hells Canyon and the Hells Canyon Creek Interpretive Center & Boat Launch

Making up the deepest river gorge in North America, Hells Canyon offers dramatic views of the Snake River as it carves the border between Oregon and Idaho. Drive the Hells Canyon Road / Idaho Power Road past the Hells Canyon Dam to the small Hells Canyon Creek Interpretive Center to learn about the canyon, its geology, flora and fauna...all while enjoying its air conditioning on a hot summer day. Short hikes down to the Oregon side of the river are available, as is seasonal viewing of bighorn sheep, mountain goats, black bears and other flora and fauna.

> Hells Canyon Creek Visitor Center
> 541-785-3395

- Open 8:00 a.m. – 4:00 p.m. Early May – to Early October
- Open Spring through Late Summer – Outdoor displays are available year-round
- Travel time to Hells Canyon from Joseph, OR is 3 hours

Driving Directions:

Drive east from Joseph for 8 miles towards Imnaha. Turn right on Wallowa Mountain Byway (USFS Road #39) and follow this to Oregon Highway 86. Turn left to Copperfield / Oxbow. Cross the bridge into Idaho at Copperfield and turn left / north onto Hells Canyon Road. Follow this for 22 miles to Hells Canyon Dam. Cross the dam and continue a little over 1 mile to the visitor center. Allow 3 hours from Joseph.

Detailed Driving Directions:

- Fill your gas tank before leaving Joseph
- Reset your odometer at the intersection of E Wallowa Ave. and Main Street in Joseph
- Leave Joseph and drive east on E Wallowa Ave., which turns into Imnaha Hwy 350
- Turn right / South onto Wallowa Mountain Road / FS-39 at 8 miles. This becomes Wallowa Mountain Loop / NF-39 at 16.7 miles
- Turn right and head south on Upper Imnaha Rd. / NF-39 at 36.2 miles
- Turn left back onto Wallowa Mountain Loop / NF-39 at 38.2 miles
- Turns into North Pine Rd. / NF-39 at 47.1 miles
- Follow North Pine Rd. / NF-39 until it connects with Hwy 86 at Mile 61.3 – Left / east goes to Copperfield, and right / west goes to Halfway, Baker City and ultimately Prairie City
- Turn left / east and head to Copperfield, OR at 68.3 miles
- Cross the bridge at Copperfield into Idaho and proceed left / north onto Hells Canyon Road / Idaho Power Road until it "officially" terminates at the dam. (90.5 Miles) Cross the dam and follow the road on the Oregon side approximately 1 mile to where it ends at the Interpretive Center

☐ Hells Canyon Activity: Hike the metal stairs of the Deep Creek Stairway Trail #218

A unique short .2 mile hike takes you from the Hells Canyon Dam down steep metal stairways to the Snake River and the mouth of Deep Creek. Expect to see fishermen here trying their luck for Chinook, Trout and Carp.

Directions: Park on the Idaho side of the Hells Canyon Dam and find the trailhead at the point the road begins to cross the dam. Follow the obvious stairs.

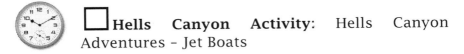

☐ **Hells Canyon Activity**: Hells Canyon Adventures – Jet Boats

Offering jet boat adventures ranging from casual tours to whitewater thrills, Hells Canyon Adventures allows you to experience the grandeur of the Snake River and Hells Canyon up close...and fast! Call or visit HellsCanyonAdventures.com for information on this year's trips, rates and availability. Note: The Snake River is closed to motorized craft on some days of the week, so plan accordingly.

- Kirkwood Tour – Offers the largest rapids with steep canyon walls – 54 Miles round trip – Boards at 10:00 a.m. – Returns between 3:00 p.m. – 4:00 p.m. – Lunch is included - Adults: $180 / person – Children 5-11: $99

- Granite Creek – Expect rushing water and steep rock walls – 16 Miles round trip – Boards at 10:00 a.m. – Returns approximately 11:45 a.m. – Also boards at 2:00 p.m. and returns approximately 4:00 p.m. - Adults: $87 / person – Children 3-11: $60

- Wild Sheep Tour – The most mellow adventure offered – 12 Miles round trip – Boards at 10:00 a.m. – Returns approximately 12:00 p.m. – Also boards at 2:00 p.m. and returns approximately 4:00 p.m. – Lunch served on the morning trip - Adults: $77 / $60 person – Children 3-11: $40 / $35.

- Call to confirm all departure times are still current
- Departs from the Hells Canyon Visitor Center & Boat Ramp
- Single day trips last 2, 4 or 6 hours
- Arrive 30 minutes prior to your departure
- Swimming stops offered in July and August

- Bring your camera and binoculars
- www.HellsCanyonAdventures.com
- JetBoat@HellsCanyonAdventures.com
- 541-785-3352

Driving Directions:

Drive east from Joseph for 8 miles towards Imnaha. Turn right on Wallowa Mountain Byway (USFS Road #39) and follow this to Oregon Highway 86. Turn left to Copperfield / Oxbow. Cross the bridge into Idaho at Copperfield and turn left / north onto Hells Canyon Road. Follow this for 22 miles to Hells Canyon Dam. Cross the dam and continue a little over 1 mile to the visitor center. Allow 3 hours from Joseph.

Return To Route:

After visiting the Hells Canyon area, you will return the way you came to Copperfield, before continuing west on the Hells Canyon Scenic Byway / Hwy 86 to Halfway and Baker City. (It is approximately 2.5 hours from Hells Canyon Dam to Baker City.) After arriving in Baker City, you'll then travel west on the Journey Through Time Scenic Byway / Hwy 7 to Whitney, OR before continuing to Prairie City, OR.

☐ Next Stop: Whitney, OR – Old Ghost Town

While traveling west on the Journey Through Time Scenic Byway, you'll come upon the ghost town of Whitney, OR. More a collection of abandoned old buildings than a town, it used to be a main stop on the Sumpter Valley Railroad line, which ran a distance of 81 miles from Baker City to Prairie City during the years of 1890 to 1947.

◻ **Next Stop**: Austin House Café & Country Store

The perfect place to stop for a meal or refreshing snacks for the road. The Austin House Café & Country Store welcomes visitors with its Eastern Oregon lodge interior offering breakfast, lunch and dinner. And to top it off, you'll find hand-dipped ice cream, milk shakes and a wealth of Huckleberry items in the form of ice cream, jelly, coffee, candles and more.

Austin House Café & Country Store
75805 US-26
Bates, OR 97817
541-448-2526

- Monday: 8:00 a.m. – 5:00 p.m.
- Tuesday & Wednesday: Closed
- Thursday: 8:00 a.m. – 5:00 p.m.
- Friday & Saturday: 8:00 a.m. – 7:00 p.m.
- Sunday: 9:00 a.m. – 5:00 p.m.

Reservations are not required, but they are suggested.

Note: The Austin House Café is open year-round, but the hours are reduced as they see fit during November – April.

www.Discover-Oregon.com

☐ **Next Stop**: Prairie City, OR

Your Discover Oregon journey finishes at Prairie City, where you'll spend your last night in the Historic Hotel Prairie.

☐ **Prairie City Stop**: DeWitt Museum Depot Park – Prairie City

 Started in 1890, the Sumpter Valley Railway carried timber, mail, passengers and supplies along an 81-mile rail route between Baker City and Prairie City until 1947. Today, the DeWitt Museum is dedicated to preserving the history of this important rail line, showcasing artifacts from its everyday existence, including photographs of its massive locomotives and some of their spectacular wrecks, rare historical documents, railway antiques, tools, lanterns and more. In addition, the museum houses a large collection of various antiques, rocks and minerals gathered by the DeWitts as they traveled the world.

DeWitt Museum Depot Park
425 South Main St
Prairie City, Oregon 97869
541-820-3330

- Open 10:00 a.m. – 5:00 p.m., Wed. through Sat.
- Open May 15th through October 15th

Driving Directions: As you drive through Prairie City, turn south onto South Main Street and follow this one third of a mile until you see the DeWitt Museum on your left.

TONIGHT'S LODGING
HISTORIC HOTEL PRAIRIE -
PRAIRIE CITY, OR

A highlight of the trip is a stay in the Historic Hotel Prairie. Built in 1910 to serve travelers to the area, as well as Sumpter Valley Railroad business clientele, this beautifully restored piece of Oregon history presents accommodations which "blend the charm of the past with the comfort of the present."

The Historic Hotel Prairie has nine rooms, including a spacious one-bedroom suite with a kitchen. All rooms include a private bath, offer cable TV and Wi-Fi, and are non-smoking.

Historic Hotel Prairie
112 Front Street
Prairie City, OR 97869
541-820-4800
HotelPrairie@ortelco.net

Note: As you travel to Prairie City, keep in mind that many of the restaurants in town close by 8:00 p.m. El Cocinero restaurant is often open until 9:00 p.m. - 541-820-4414.

Driving Directions: Located in the heart of Prairie City, at the corner of Front Street and S. Main Street.

Lodging Option #1: Riverside School House B & B

Yes, this is a quaint B & B inside an old school house! Voted as one of the best places to stay in Oregon B & Bs, the historical Riverside School House is divided into two large suites, separated by French doors. The front suite has a queen and a double bed, bathroom and a small kitchen, while the rear suite has a small sitting room, a bedroom with a queen bed and a bathroom.

To ensure privacy, only one party may rent the school house at a time, whether you rent the front suite, rear suite or both.

Riverside School House B & B
28076 North River Road
Prairie City, OR 97869
541-820-4731
www.RiversideSchoolHouse.com

Note: The best way to make reservations or to receive information is via email at: RiversideRanchpcor@Gmail.com

Driving Directions: From the intersection of Hwy 26 and Main Street in Prairie City, drive south on South Main Street past the DeWitt Museum before turning left onto SW Bridge Street. Follow this as it turns into Summit Prairie Road/County Road 62 until you see a left turn for North River Road/County Road

61 (6.5 Miles from Prairie City) Turn left / west here and follow this ¼ mile to the Riverside School House B & B on the right.

Lodging Option #2: Pine Shadows Getaway

 Located 10.5 miles southeast of Prairie City, Pine Shadows Getaway offers a small collection of luxurious cabins tucked under old growth Pines and Firs next to the headwaters of the John Day River. Inside each cabin, guests will find clean high-end amenities, including comfortable furniture, well-appointed kitchens, rain shower heads, lush towels, artisan soaps, and beds featuring down comforters and soft 600 thread count sheets. Outside, guests can fly fish, lie in a hammock, enjoy a spa, or sit around a fire ring while roasting marshmallows.

Pine Shadows Getaway Resort
25923 Green Haven Road
Prairie City, OR 97869
541-820-3736
PineShadowGetaway@gmail.com

- Open May 1st – October 1st.
- *Note: There is a 2 night minimum stay at the Pine Shadows Getaway, so if you choose to stay here, you'll need to add an additional day to your trip schedule.*

Driving Directions: From the intersection of Hwy 26 and Main Street in Prairie City, drive south on South Main Street past the DeWitt Museum before turning left onto SW Bridge Street. Follow this as it turns into Summit Prairie Road/County Road 62 for 10.5 miles until you see a sign on your left for Green Haven Rd. Turn left onto the gravel road, cross the river and Pine Shadows Getaway Resort will be the first gate on the left.

www.Discover-Oregon.com

Notes

DAY TEN

PRAIRIE CITY TO HOME

"Oregon is an inspiration. Whether you come to it, or are born to it, you are entranced by our state's beauty, the opportunity she affords, and the independent spirit of her citizens."

Governor Tom McCall

DAY 10
PRAIRIE CITY TO HOME

Sheep Rock, Journey Through Time Oregon Scenic Byway

Day 10 – Date: /   /

Summary: Where You're Going Today

- Home

Today, your *Oregon Road Trips – Northeast Edition* is finished! Choose your route home and cherish your new memories. But first, begin your day with breakfast at Chuck's Little Diner in Prairie City.

☐ Prairie City Restaurant: Chuck's Little Diner

Start your day traveling home with a breakfast at Chuck's Little Diner, conveniently located a few doors down from the Historic Hotel Prairie on Main Street. Popular with locals, it serves ranch style breakfasts of fluffy pancakes, hash browns, bacon, sausage, homemade flaky biscuits and eggs just the way you like them.

Chuck's Little Diner
Breakfast and Lunch
142 Front Street
Prairie City, OR 97869

Our Recommendations on How to Travel Home:

If you're heading home towards **Mt. Hood, Portland** and points north, we recommend you drive west on Hwy 26 from Prairie City and turn north onto Hwy 19, towards Shaniko and Maupin, much of which travels amidst the impressive geologic wonders of the Journey Through Time Oregon Scenic Byway. It's a bit slower of a route, but far more scenic.

If you're heading towards **Central Oregon, Southern Oregon or the Willamette Valley**, we recommend you continue on Hwy 26 west towards Prineville, passing by the Painted Hills, the small town of Mitchell, and Stein's Pillar. This route takes you through some beautiful Oregon country.

Note: As you travel home from Prairie City, you'll actually be traveling along much of Day 1 in our book *Oregon Road Trips – Southeast Edition.*

Highlights of Day 1 include the Kam Wah Chung Museum in John Day, the Thomas Condon Paleontology Center and the grandeur of the Journey Through Time Oregon Scenic Byway. For complete details, pick up our book, *Oregon Road Trips – Southeast Edition* and start your next grand Oregon adventure!

www.Discover-Oregon.com

US Army Corps of Engineers ®
Portland District

AVERAGE MONTHLY FISH COUNT AT BONNEVILLE DAM

Here are the average monthly fish counts of common adult fish that pass Bonneville Lock and Dam. These fish are unique because they are anadromous (they begin their lives in fresh water, spend part of their life in the ocean, and return to fresh water to spawn). The majority of fish migrating upstream past Bonneville do so between March and November each year. The following numbers represent the ten year monthly average from 2006-2015.

Month	CHINOOK* SALMON (KING)	SOCKEYE SALMON (BLUEBACK)	COHO* SALMON (SILVER)	STEELHEAD TROUT	SHAD	LAMPREY
January	1	0	0	543	0	0
February	3	0	0	387	0	0
March	363	0	0	1,479	0	0
April	54,569	0	0	1,361	0	0
May	116,352	84	0	1,727	240,876	787
June	79,770	193,212	0	9,502	1,907,935	5,133
July	37,564	91,374	2	87,796	113,624	10,706
August	111,089	442	10,266	154,124	272	4,386
September	429,914	13	71,599	76,994	0	1,190
October	43,332	0	46,645	10,874	0	64
November	2,117	0	5,466	1,937	0	19
December	53	0	183	779	0	1

* Jacks included

Fish climbing the fish ladder can either jump over the walls that separate pools in the ladders, or swim through holes in the walls.

www.Discover-Oregon.com

Phone Numbers - Oregon Road Trips NE Edition

- 1910 Historic Enterprise House: 541-426-4238
- Balch Hotel: 541-467-2277
- Bronze Antler Bed & Breakfast: 541-432-0230
- Columbia River Sternwheeler: 503-224-3900
- Condon Hotel: 541-384-4624
- Eagle Cap Ranger District Office: 541-426-4978
- Eagle Cap Wilderness Train: 800-323-7300
- El Cocinero Restaurant – Prairie City: 541-820-4414
- Geiser Grand Hotel: 541-523-1889
- Hells Canyon Jet Boat: 541-785-3352
- Historic Hotel Prairie: 541-820-4800
- Historic Union Hotel: 541-562-1200
- Hot Lake Springs Resort & Hotel: 541-963-4685
- Joseph Branch Railriders: 541-786-6149
- Joseph Forest Service Visitor Center: 541-426-5546
- Les Schwab Tire Center – Baker City – 541-523-3679
- Les Schwab Tire Center – Enterprise – 541-426-3139
- Les Schwab Tire Center – Heppner – 541-676-9481
- Les Schwab Tire Center – John Day – 541- 575-1346
- Les Schwab Tire Center – La Grande – 541-963-8411
- Oregon Dept. of Transportation: 800-977-6368
- Summit Grill – Wallowas: 541-432-5331
- Sumpter Valley Railroad: 541-894-2268
- Sunrise Iron Antique Tractors: 541-426-4407
- Valley Bronze Gallery / Foundry: 541-432-7445
- Wallowa Lake Lodge & Cabins: 541-432-9821
- Wallowa Lake Marina: 541-432-9115
- Wallowa Lake Tramway: 541-432-5331
- Wallowa Lake – Summit Grill: 541-432-5331
- Wallowa Whitman Ranger Station: 541-523-6391
- Zumwalt Prairie Nature Conservancy: 541-426-3458

AND ANOTHER GREAT ROAD TRIP IS READY!

Oregon Road Trips – Southeast Edition

If you enjoyed this road trip, then you're sure to enjoy exploring remote Southeast Oregon. As with this title, you'll simply turn each page as you motor along and choose which points of interest to stop at and explore during your day's journey, *all while making your way toward that evening's lodging in a historic Oregon hotel.*

You'll drive to the top of 9,734' Steens Mountain, stay in the 1923 Frenchglen Hotel, explore the remote Leslie Gulch, see how stage coaches are built, dig for fossils, hike "Crack in the Ground", look for wild Mustangs, eat at a truly unique and remote Oregon restaurant, marvel at the geologic wonders of the Journey Through Time Scenic Byway and so much more!

Available Now at Retailers
Throughout Oregon and Online

NOW ENJOY AN
OREGON COAST ROAD TRIP!

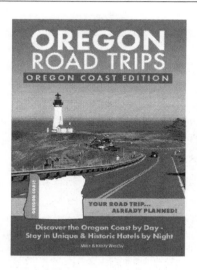

Oregon Road Trips – Oregon Coast Edition

Pack your bags, because you're about to explore the grandeur of Oregon's dramatic coastline during an adventurous 9-day road trip from Astoria south to Brookings. You'll journey along Oregon's beautiful Highway 101 as you discover countless scenic beaches, tour historic lighthouses, wander through quaint beach towns, watch whales spouting just off shore, ride in the cab of a 1925 steam locomotive, eat tasty Dungeness Crab fresh off the boat...or catch your own, stay in historic hotels, explore unique shops, meet friendly people and so much more!

Your perfect Oregon Coast road trip awaits!

Available Now at Retailers
Throughout Oregon and Online

DISCOVER THE COLUMBIA RIVER GORGE!

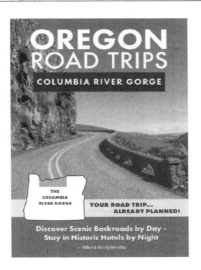

Oregon Road Trips – Columbia River Gorge Edition

Journey along the Historic Columbia River Highway deep into the Columbia River Gorge, where you'll spend 5 days seeing the Gorge's majestic waterfalls, flying in a vintage 2-seater biplane, hiking through the historic Mosier Tunnels, stepping into the void on an exciting zip line tour, walking amidst the Gorge's beautiful spring wildflowers, finding your next book at Oregon's oldest bookstore, and even spotting Giraffes, Zebras, Camels, Ostriches and more!

Your perfect Columbia River Gorge road trip awaits, and it's already planned for you!

Available Now at Retailers
Throughout Oregon and Online

ROAD TRIP OREGON'S MAJESTIC MT. HOOD!

Oregon Road Trips – Mt. Hood Edition
Via the Columbia River Gorge

An alpine Oregon Road Trip adventure is waiting for you!

Set out on an exciting Oregon road trip where every night ends at a charming historic hotel, finishing with majestic Timberline Lodge at 6,000' on the south slope of Mt. Hood! Explore the Historic Columbia River Highway, hike the unique Mosier Tunnels route, visit Oregon's oldest bookstore, walk among the Columbia River Gorge's colorful spring wildflowers, fly in a vintage 2-seater biplane, ride to over 7,000' on the Magic Mile Chairlift, discover the rustic and remote 1889 Cloud Cap Inn on Mt. Hood's eastern flank, and so much more.

Available Now at Retailers
Throughout Oregon and Online

Southwest Oregon Awaits!

Oregon Road Trips – Southwest Edition

Visit 13 historic covered bridges, spend a night in Crater Lake Lodge, discover a vintage aircraft museum, enjoy a play in Ashland, explore deep into the Oregon Caves, wander an Oregon ghost town, see some of Oregon's most beautiful waterfalls, tour the Applegate Wine Trail, and so much more on your 9-day road trip through Southwest Oregon. As with our other Oregon Road Trip books, you'll simply motor along while you discover Oregon, and finish each night at a unique historic hotel!

Your Southwest Oregon road trip awaits, and it's already planned for you!

Available Now at Retailers
Throughout Oregon and Online

What to See, Do & Explore on the Oregon Coast!

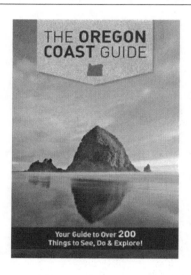

At 363 miles long, Oregon's scenic coastline is filled with countless natural wonders and attractions to see, do, and explore. Hike to a high bluff to watch for whales, walk a long sandy beach, explore a historic lighthouse, catch a live Dungeness crab, join in the fun of a sandcastle building contest, even ride aboard an old-fashioned steam train. The problem is...how do you uncover all of these activities to get the most out of your trip? The solution is the new *Oregon Coast Guide*. Inside these pages, you'll discover over 200 fun and adventurous things to see, do and explore while visiting the Oregon Coast, complete with descriptions, photos, maps, tips, a whale watching guide and much more.

Available Now at Retailers
Throughout Oregon and Online

About the Authors

Mike & Kristy Westby – Atop Steens Mountain

Having been to all six "corners" of Oregon...North, South, East, West, Top and Bottom, (The top of Mt. Hood and the Oregon Coast) we decided it would be fun to take off on a series of multi-day road trips throughout the state. During our travels, we were surprised at the number of folks we met along the way who said they've always wanted to do the same thing, but they didn't know where to even begin planning such a trip. How do you find interesting places? What routes do you take? How do separate it all into even days, all while ending each day at a historic hotel? With that in mind, we decided to write our road trip guides so other like-minded souls can easily benefit from the knowledge we've gleaned over the years and set out on their own adventures.

We'd love to hear about the journeys you've taken with our different road trip guides, so feel free to drop us a note anytime or send us a photo, especially if you're on the road!

ContactUs@Discover-Oregon.com

WE RECOMMEND...

Restore Oregon

As you journeyed through Northeast Oregon, you no doubt noticed the many historic structures which capture the history and culture of our state. Many, however, are in urgent need of protection and preservation. Restore Oregon

SAVING HISTORIC PLACES

is dedicated to "taking care of the places that make Oregon, OREGON" and preserving them for future generations. Learn more at RestoreOregon.org

The Nature of Bend

Written by LeeAnn Kriegh, The Nature of Bend is a nature guide like no other. Funny, informative, and filled with local flavor, it's the one book you need to identify, locate and learn about more than 350 plants and animals across Central Oregon. Available at bookstores, coffee shops and elsewhere in Central Oregon. Learn more at NatureofBend.com

Les Schwab Tire Centers

If you're on the road and have a flat tire, brake issues or a similar problem, we highly recommend the

very helpful and nice folks at your nearby Les Schwab Tire Center. Located throughout Oregon. Find phone numbers for multiple locations on Page 150.

Building The Columbia River Highway

The intriguing story of how visionary artists, poets and engineers came together to forge a route through the mighty Columbia River Gorge and create the nation's first scenic highway, a "poem in stone." Ride along with author Peg Willis as she explores the beginnings of this miracle highway, the men who created it, and the obstacles they overcame on the road to its completion.

Antiques & Oddities

A Columbia River Gorge "destination" for over 20 years, Antiques & Oddities in Bingen, WA is home to an eclectic collection of quality antiques from near and far, including Asia and Europe.

211 W. Steuben St., Bingen, WA
509-493-4242

Are You a Disney Fan?

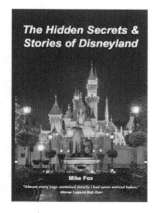

Enjoy three great books that reveal 100s of hidden secrets, which the Disney Imagineers have purposely hidden for park guests to find and enjoy; 1) *The Hidden Secrets & Stories of Disneyland*, 2) *Disneyland In-Depth*, and 3) *The Hidden Secrets & Stories of Walt Disney World*.

Available online, as well as at the prestigious Walt Disney Family Museum and the Walt Disney Hometown Museum.

Made in the USA
San Bernardino, CA
29 December 2018